Keith Brymer Jones is a British potter and ceramic designer, internationally known for his homeware 'Word' range and celebrated as the lead judge on *The Great Pottery Throwdown*, Love Productions television series for Channel Four and HBO. In February 2021, the *Evening Standard* described him as 'Quite simply the best person on TV at this present moment in time'.

After an apprenticeship at Harefield Pottery, he started hand-making ceramics for retailers including the Conran Group, Habitat, Barneys New York, Monsoon, Laura Ashley and Heals. As Head of Design for MAKE International he collaborates with other designers including Jane Foster, Scion Living, Hokolo and many more.

BOY IN A CHINA SHOP

Life, Clay and Everything

KEITH BRYMER JONES
With Michael James

HODDER

First published in Great Britain in 2022 by Hodder & Stoughton
An Hachette UK company

This paperback edition published in 2023

4

A CIP catalogue record for this title is available from the British Library

Paperback ISBN 9781529385250
eBook ISBN 9781529385236

Typeset in Bembo by Hewer Text UK Ltd, Edinburgh
Printed and bound in Great Britain by Clays Ltd, Elcograf S.p.A.

Hodder & Stoughton policy is to use papers that are natural, renewable
and recyclable products and made from wood grown in sustainable
forests. The logging and manufacturing processes are expected to
conform to the environmental regulations of the country of origin.

Hodder & Stoughton Ltd
Carmelite House
50 Victoria Embankment
London EC4Y 0DZ

www.hodder.co.uk

I would like to dedicate this book to my wonderful son Ned…
if you take the time to read it,
you may learn a little bit more about me,
and in turn about yourself.

xx

CONTENTS

1

THAT SATISFYING THUMP

It all starts with a ball of clay. That satisfying thump as I slap it down onto the centre of the wheel. Is there a better sound in the world? It's a process I have been through thousands and thousands of times before, but it still gives me the same thrill, the same wave of anticipation hits me as I consider what I will create in the next couple of minutes. After forty-four years at this game, I can tell by gently squeezing the clay if it will be an easy throwing session or whether I am going to have to work harder to manipulate the clay. Either way, this is when the magic begins. The combination of a spinning wheel and two hands transforming clay into a bowl, a plate, a mug or anything else I choose *is* a magical process. I still marvel at it.

With the wheel spinning at its fastest speed, I centre the clay. With my hands either side I apply a little pressure with the heels of my palms, drawing it upwards to form a cone. Working from the thicker base, I increase the pressure, then ease it off as I pull it upwards to a point. I gently massage the clay up and down, visualising all those clay particles working their way round in the same direction, stretching it out, making it more pliable. When the clay feels ready, I plunge my hand into my water bucket, pour a little over the centred ball and get to work.

For me, the bowl form is the most satisfying shape to make. I see them as the ceramic equivalent of cupped hands, offering something to a stranger. The embodiment of all that is good in human nature, they are what we use when we want to share food with friends and family. Bowls would have been one of the first shapes thrown by humans; before cutlery they were the most practical object from which to eat. I think the bowl might be the very first design classic.

Before making a bowl, as I centre the clay, I visualise it in my head. I know what height and width it is going to be, how curved the sides will be. I mentally rehearse every move I am going to make. Then I start, pressing my middle finger into the centre of the clay, drawing it outwards to create a smooth crater. Next, positioning my body over the bowl, I form crab-like pincers with both hands, place them over the rim farthest from me and with my fingers on the outside, thumbs inside, I apply some pressure to the clay, steadily drawing my hands upwards to form the side of the bowl. Before doing this I'll slow the wheel down; if I don't the clay will 'collar up', or stretch outwards rather than upwards.

All this I do instinctively, as naturally as I breathe. My hands automatically move into the correct position, making minute adjustments when and where they are required, adding a little water here and there so my hands glide across the surface. It's all about lightness of touch, making just enough contact with the clay as it spins round, so it will obediently follow where I direct it. It's an extremely tactile, sensual experience and I don't mind admitting that I am addicted to it. The connection is so profound, it's like the clay is an extension of me.

It's all over in a flash. I think that's another integral part of the process that I find so appealing. It has to be done at speed, in one continuous movement; there's no time to stop and think about it, it is two or three minutes of total concentration. The best part of it is that when I've finished, I can pick up another lump of clay and do it again and again.

This was how I kept myself sane during the first Covid-19 lockdown in 2020: doing what I love most. Of course, for the first few days my partner Marj and I didn't know what to do with ourselves. We had no reference points. We had never seen shops, pubs and restaurants shut down en masse before, and no one had ever forbidden us to see our friends and family – or anyone else, for that matter. It was unnerving. But after those first tense days I stopped stressing about work, and then stopped stressing about everything. That was a first for me. It seemed there was no point worrying about deadlines and projects that had all become meaningless in this strange, limbo-like world. None of it mattered while so many people were dying. All we had to do was stay home for a bit.

So I settled into a nice little routine. I'd get up a good hour or two after my usual waking hour, enjoy a leisurely breakfast (something previously totally unknown to me), and then sit down at my wheel to centre some clay and make something just for the hell of it. I would experiment, too; anything and everything was on the cards. Pure experimentation was something I had not really indulged in for nearly forty years. And it was brilliant. With no time constraints, no one on the phone trying to hurry me up and no pressure, a strange thing happened to me. Marj noticed it one afternoon after I'd woken from a nap.

'Blimey. You're relaxed,' she said.

I checked my pulse. She was right. I was. Probably for the first time in years.

After a few weeks of this, Marj, seeing that I had built up a nice little collection of mugs and bowls and other pieces for my own amusement, put in an unusual request. She asked if I could make her a dinner service. What a novel idea, I thought: making something for my own use. I'd never done it before. In the past I'd made things for friends, but never for myself. We love entertaining. Marj is a great cook and though it didn't bother either of us that we used odd plates and bowls when we had guests, the thought of having special ones for those occasions really appealed to me. I told her that I would get right on it.

Being able to spend loads of time with my favourite person in the world was certainly another benefit of lockdown. Marj is my muse, and I never thought I would get to say that about someone. She inspires me every day, and I have never met anyone so talented in so many ways. She can sing, act, make clothes and bags, cook like a dream and, crucially, is brilliant at being my best friend. It has made such a difference to my life having someone I can open up to, a person I can trust with my fears, weaknesses and vulnerability, and know they will never take advantage of them.

Marj and I met at that most romantic of places, a trade fair, in lovely Harrogate. She was standing on a grassy knoll wearing a green polka-dot dress and the sight of her stopped me in my tracks. I told her she looked nice. Throughout my life I have not been shy of handing out compliments to people, male or female, if I feel they deserve it. It costs nothing and may make someone feel better about themselves. I get the odd person who takes it the wrong way, but all I am doing is being honest, I have no other agenda … usually. This time was different. I had to get to know this person. And I did. Lucky me.

So, early lockdown was a bit of a treat for us, and a chance to spend some time together. We played silly games and got used to Zoom, experimented with clay and stood in queues, cursed toilet-roll hoarders and learned to perfect our baking (in Marj's case – I'm useless with food).

Marj and I would go for our regulation short walks every day along the beach at Margate or Seasalter, look out over the water and remind ourselves how lucky we were. At least we lived in a place with fresh air, open space and blue horizons.

There was little I could do, in the circumstances, but continue to hunker down on the north Kent coast with Marj, my clay and Radio 4. Something I found myself listening to with almost religious zeal was *A History of the World in 100 Objects*. There was something in presenter Neil MacGregor's voice, and the accompanying music, that reminded me of watching educational programmes at school in the 1970s. Yes, it was comforting.

Unsurprisingly, perhaps, I paid most attention to those episodes that dealt with ceramics. I find pots have a unique storytelling essence of their own, in terms of telling us how our ancestors lived. Pottery is the oldest of handicrafts, and for archaeologists, digging up ceramics is like finding lost letters in the attic. They can tell us how the people who made them lived and died, and sometimes they can tell us a lot more.

Take object number 64, for example, known rather uninspiringly as 'The David Vases'. Ignore the name: these exquisite pieces, over two feet high, encapsulate everything I have come to love about ceramics; they are timeless and perfect, maybe too precious to have ever been used and discarded, to be dug up centuries later. They are the oldest and probably best-known blue and white porcelain objects in the world. The dedication inscribed on them tells us they were made in China on Tuesday 13 May 1351 by Zhang Wenjin, who presented them to a temple in what is now Wuyuan. Yes, that's Wuyuan, not to be confused with nearby Wuhan, now famous for a very different reason.

Zhang Wenjin gave them to the temple, so that they could be dedicated to the gods, in return for protection. They were originally a set of three, but sadly the accompanying incense burner has not been found – yet. And the name? Well, somewhat prosaically, they are named after Sir Percival David, who bought them as the crowning glory to his vast Chinese ceramic collection, which is now on display in the British Museum.

Porcelain looms large in my own history. The material itself never ceases to amaze me. The finish of the David Vases, white porcelain with a cobalt-blue underglaze, is what we think of as being classically Chinese, but the technique actually originated in Persia, modern-day Iran. The reason for this misconception can be laid squarely at the feet of thirteenth-century uber-nutter, Genghis Khan. The devastation he dealt out during his Mongol Invasions laid waste to the Middle East pottery industry, with Persia particularly badly affected.

Luckily for the rest of the world, his grandson Kublai Khan had no time for war – or anything else, for that matter, with a harem of 7,000. On becoming emperor of China in 1260, he sought peace and prosperity. A great supporter of the arts, he encouraged the manufacture of luxury goods and the conquered lands became major markets for these. Blue and white ware had long been popular in Persia, so the Chinese sent products there that suited local taste. Their potters achieved this by using the Persian-sourced pigment cobalt – known as 'Muslim blue' – to get the distinctive shade still recognisable today.

Blue and white porcelain then became popular back in China, too. Have you ever thought about where the word 'porcelain' comes from, though? Well, it's European. The great Venetian merchant and explorer Marco Polo travelled extensively through Asia along the Silk Road, an ancient trade route that linked the Roman Empire and China. Coming back to Venice, he eulogised about the amazing blue and white ceramics he had seen. He compared their lustre and appearance to cowrie shells. Now, Venetians called cowrie shells *porcellana* (slang for little curled-up piglets) – and so the term porcelain was coined. So blue and white porcelain, perceived to be Chinese through and through, is actually Persian, and was named by a Venetian.

I could not get enough of these stories about inanimate objects, all squeezed into fifteen fascinating minutes. I was learning about history without realising it and the information seeped into my pores. I would find myself regaling Marj with more and more stories about objects. Maybe I'm getting old – no, I'm definitely getting old – but my love of craftsmanship, beauty and creativity keeps getting stronger. I'm a people person, but I'm also an inanimate object person. The permanence of artefacts – the fact that people have always found ways of making beautiful things, and those things can survive centuries and tell us stories – both grounds me and inspires me.

So if we choose to make something, like any of those choices we can make in life, it can have reverberations not only through our own lives, but in those of people we have never met, and those who haven't yet been born.

All a bit mind-blowing, eh?

2
'COME ON!
CONCENTRATE BOY!'

There is a Welsh saying that goes … wait for it … 'Ara bach a bob yn dipyn mae sdicio bys i din gwybedyn.' This translates, and you'll be pleased you read this, as, 'You have to take it very slowly, and bit by bit, to get your finger up a fly's arse.' Charming!

Clearly, it is a rather odd way of expressing that old adage that patience is a virtue, and beautifully illustrates what a singular, characterful folk the Welsh are. If I were allowed a couple of words to sum up my attitude to my career, patient would have to be the first one, and single-minded the second. I may not appear a patient man, but once I set my heart on something, I am dogged in pursuing it. Unlike most of my friends, who seem to have flitted happily from one job to another, or sometimes not so happily, I have stuck at the same thing for nearly forty years.

An awful lot of that time has been spent waiting: for clay to dry, for the kiln to cool down, for the invoices to be paid. Then there was all the patience required to acquire the skills, techniques and haptic ability – the sense of touch – that has enabled me to get the clay to do what I want. It took years of watching, listening, learning and practising.

I have always absorbed professional knowledge from whomever, wherever and whenever I can. I am a bit of a pottery technique sponge in that respect. But I have to say, for me the most striking, earth-shattering conveyor of knowledge on the subject has to be a short black-and-white film, which was cheaply made, and looks like it could have been made a hundred years ago, on the moon. It features an old man nearing the end of his working life, going about his daily business. He sits at a potter's wheel while another man feeds him balls of clay. He puffs away on a pipe as he works, throwing pots with astonishing speed and dexterity, at the rate of about one every twenty seconds. Think about that. This man is a master, totally in control of, and at ease with, his craft.

His name was Isaac Button. I cannot remember where or when I first saw this film, as for many years the only places you could see it would be pottery or craft museums. But viewing Isaac Button in the flesh, so to speak, was immense for me as I'd heard so much about him; it was like seeing a mythical hero – a pottery Superman – coming up the garden path. If there was one potter I desperately wanted to emulate, it was him.

Button worked his whole life at Soil Hill, a pottery bought by his grandfather in 1897. In those days, it sat on a windswept hillside outside Halifax alongside a dozen or so other potteries. By 1943, when it was passed on to Isaac and his brother Arthur, it was one of the last few surviving. For some reason, no one knows why, the brothers fell out and Isaac, unable to find a suitable apprentice, decided to work the place on his own – for the next eighteen years. What he did during those years was astonishing.

He would dig the clay from the local hillside himself, and routinely use a ton of it every day. Then he would throw; hundreds of pots at a sitting, at a breakneck pace. He had to keep his 500-cubic-foot kiln stoked with two and a half tons of coal, and a firing would keep him up for forty-eight hours straight. His products were simple ware for everyday use: jugs, jars, bowls, butter-dishes, casseroles and flowerpots. They were not avant-garde, and they were not noticeable. They spoke of tradition, masterly skill, and bloody hard work.

But why am I telling you all this now? That film of Isaac Button was made in 1965 by photographer John Anderson and Robert Fournier, a founder member of the Craftsmen Potters Association. They knew Button's retirement later that year would end 200 years of pot making at Soil Hill, and they wanted to document a dying art, that of the English country potter. It so happens that 1965 was the year I was born. For me, there is significance in him bowing out as I entered the world. I feel, in some way, like a connection was made and a torch passed on.

★ ★ ★

I grew up in north London, but my family background is Welsh to the core – hence the tongue-twisting quote. My paternal grandmother came from a wealthy family. Her father, Owen Picton Davies, was a bit of a 1920s mover and shaker. Born in Carmarthenshire, he moved to London in his early twenties and was influential in founding the Young Wales Association (YWA) in 1920, a social and political hub for Welsh people living in London. He was President of the London Welsh Trust from 1928–30 (a post held later by David Lloyd George) and he stood as a Liberal candidate for Clapham in the 1929 General Election, although he failed to be elected. He then served as High Sheriff of Carmarthenshire from 1934 to 1935, moving his family to a grand old house called Castell Pigyn.

My father was evacuated there during the war, and learned to speak Welsh during his stay. The house remained in the family after Owen's death but, as so often with old, rambling mansions that are expensive to maintain, it 'went on fire' and burned to the ground in 1970. I can remember visiting the remains a few years later and getting that chilling, spooky feeling that house ruins always give off. The YWA was renamed the London Welsh Association and my grandfather and father both became active members, although their interest in it was sporting, not political.

My parents met in a Welsh Presbyterian church on Shaftesbury Avenue, which later became the Limelight nightclub. Naturally, they both sang in the choir and after practice they would often nip into Soho to a coffee bar like the 2i's, where my father would get up and sing along with a skiffle group or two. I find it hard to picture now. They got married on April Fool's Day 1961, and quickly started a family. My sister was born in 1962 and I followed two and a bit years later. I was a very long baby and came out elbow first – with my arm wrapped around my head – which initially caused a bit of a panic. It was a lot of fuss over nothing though, as I was only scratching my ear, the left one, with my right hand, which I still do to this day.

We lived in Woodside Park, north London, which was originally conceived as a model Garden Suburb in the 1930s. As you might imagine, it was a solidly middle-class area with the feel of a village, even though it was in the London Borough of Barnet. During the day, when the men were out at work, there were few cars parked on our street, Walmington Fold (even the name sounds warm and cosy, if not a little cloying, don't you think?). After school, this space belonged to us, and my sister and I and the neighbour's children would play without a care until we were called in for tea.

Sometimes, in summer, we would go down to Dollis Brook, a stream that flows past the bottoms of the gardens there. We would paddle in the shallow water and dig the thick clay mud on its banks to fashion crude pots, which would dry out and crack in the sun. From the age of eight, I would be allowed to go off with my best friend Tim on long bike rides along the brook, sometimes as far as Brent, seven miles away. We would be out all day long and our parents wouldn't bat an eyelid. I don't think it ever entered their minds that something untoward might happen to us in lovely, safe Woodside Park. And luckily for us, it didn't.

Tim and I met in nursery school. He stood out even at that age. Where most of us would fight over the cowboy outfit in the dressing-up box, he would go for the Native American headdress and tunic. I remember him sitting in the costume one afternoon during art class, when the teacher asked us to paint 'something nice'. Tim promptly took hold of a large paint brush, smothered it in red paint and covered several sheets of paper with it. Then, he scrunched them up and arranged them into a pile. The teacher didn't know what to make of the mess, but Tim calmly explained it was his camp fire burning brightly and keeping him warm. After that I was always in awe of 'Big Chief Tim' and his wild imagination. We became firm friends, and still are.

Frith Manor, my school, was close enough for me to walk to from home. I liked it there. My class teacher, Mr Stringer, was incredible. He would act out little scenarios during assembly to teach us how to be polite and do things 'properly'. One morning, we filed in to find him seated onstage at a table set for dinner, complete with tablecloth, plates and cutlery – though no food. He proceeded to show us how to eat properly, how to cut up food, and where to place your knife and fork once you had finished. He kept up a running commentary throughout. It is extraordinary to think of it now, like something that would have happened in Victorian times, not the 1970s in London.

My sister and I were close as children, with just over two years between us, and we'd play happily together, building camps in our back garden or making up silly games. One involved us playing 'grown-ups', with each of us in character – much like Mr Stringer, come to think of it. I became 'Mr Summonsay' and Sarah would be 'Mrs Salideedees'. She would invite me over for tea or I would take her on a boating trip and we would play out these little dramas.

I remember we had a bit of a catchphrase, for when anything went wrong. If 'Mr Summonsay' dropped something or 'Mrs Salideedees' tripped over our pet cat Rumble, we would both turn to each other and say: 'Oh! Pretend that didn't happen.' Then we'd burst out laughing and carry on with the game. When I think of this, it hits home how innocent we were. There were few distractions for children in those days; very little TV was aimed at us, so by and large we made our own entertainment and were content to do so.

The only jarring note in my childhood was the behaviour of my father. More often than not he was grumpy around the house and my sister and I tended to keep out of his way; from a young age we were aware these moods were work-related. He had started out in shipping insurance, but throughout my primary school years I remember him as the manager of the Yorkshire Building Society in Hampstead Garden Suburb. It was a well-paid job, providing us with a comfortable standard of living, but he hated it. He was anti-establishment, but at the same time had a strong work ethic inherited from his father: get yourself a good, solid, respectable job and stick to it.

It was a paradox he never came to terms with; his temperament and principles always got in the way of any career development. He resigned from the Yorkshire when his manager pointed out he was giving out too many mortgages and that was against company policy. Then he became an estate agent, perhaps the only honest one in north London. He would routinely say to people looking round a property something like: 'Don't buy this hovel, madam, the neighbours are nutters and there are rats in the skirting boards.'

Sport was the only thing that made him truly happy, both watching it and playing it. Throughout my childhood he was absent on a Saturday, either playing football for London Welsh, or tennis during the summer. The only exceptions would be when we were on holiday, or when Wimbledon was on and he would take my sister and me to watch the tennis. He was a talented player himself, competing at county level; he belonged to Brampton Tennis Club in Hendon, where he won the men's singles title year after year – he even played at Wimbledon in the under-21's tournament.

He hated paying to get in anywhere, in fact he had an aversion to doing anything by the book – a trait that has rubbed off on me. He would stride up to the VIP entrance at Wimbledon and brazenly walk in. 'If anyone asks, you're with me,' he would whisper to us out of the side of his mouth. For us, this was marvellously exciting, getting in for nothing with our 'important' father. We would then spend the day watching the matches on the outer courts, where you didn't need tickets.

His parents lived nearby, so I spent a lot of time at their house as a child. 'Pa' and 'Ma', we called them. Pa, William Brymer Jones, was an immensely proud Welshman with a real old-fashioned, no-nonsense presence about him; he was the polar opposite of politically correct, always believing he was right, but lovable with it. I remember one afternoon watching television with him. The children's show *Crackerjack* was on and there was a piece on ballet. At this point some boys were dancing onscreen and Pa turned to me.

'Look at those boys,' he said, looking appalled, and then at me. 'Bloody poofs, aren't they?'

I remember feeling awkward and giving him a dumb, nervous smile. You see, by now I was a dancer, too, and Pa knew this. His stark comment was his way of making sure I knew he didn't approve; football was for boys, dancing was for girls. It was black and white. No argument.

Luckily, my mother disagreed. She had loved dance when she was a girl and was keen on my sister and me learning, so she had enrolled us at the Kathleen Hughes School for Dancing at a very young age; I started dance classes when I was three and kept it up until I was about sixteen. We were both very competent dancers and there was serious talk of me going on to audition for ballet school when I was very young and springy. Sadly, our bodies grew into the wrong shape to take up dance as a profession. It's not that we were overweight – we were fit and healthy, but a bit too strapping.

Classes were two evenings a week, with anything between fifteen and thirty of us crammed into a hall. Mostly girls, of course. I was aware that dance was a bit of a weird thing for boys to do – and Pa would remind me, if there was ever any doubt – so I never shared that part of my life with any friends outside of dancing. But it was something I genuinely loved. It was bloody hard work, though. You would start a class by limbering up, jumping on the spot, stretching, doing lunges and skipping. We were taught how and when to breathe while we moved around the room. It was all about technique, making it look effortless. That was a big lesson, which would resonate throughout my life. You must practise hard enough so it looks as if you're not trying.

Once we had warmed up, we'd split into groups depending on what dance was on that evening. It might be the Highland fling or the sword dance. Our teacher, Melody, was the daughter of Kathleen Hughes and she had the perfect dance build. She was tiny, but so incredibly strong; boy, could she get some elevation when dancing the fling. There would be a huge smile on her face as she demonstrated for us, as if she were performing to a West End audience rather than a bunch of kids. Melody was not the sort of teacher to bawl you out for doing something wrong; she would gently explain how you might do it better. And more often than not, you did.

Her mother was different, exuding an old-school glamour and authority. You'd do anything to avoid one of her disapproving stares. She would regally parade up and down during barre exercises, with her cane at the ready. This was not for beating us with, simply to indicate those vital, minor adjustments.

'Make sure that heel is facing the ceiling,' she would cry out, as I extended my leg upwards as far as I thought it would go.

'Come on! Concentrate boy!' She would hold the cane an inch or two higher and I would strain every fibre in my skinny little legs to reach it.

We were all working towards Highland dance competitions. These were mega events, with 600–700 children and teenagers turning out. We would get up really early on a Saturday, at 6.30 a.m. and pile everything into my mother's Mini Clubman.

Our outfits would take up most of the room. You'd have a different one for each dance and between Sarah and me, we'd have more than ten outfits onboard. It must have cost my parents a fortune, particularly as we were constantly growing. We'd also have to find space for my mother's packed lunches – dancing was hungry work (not that we needed any excuse to tuck into the amazing pies and cakes my mother made). Often, we'd give lifts to other children, so it'd be a right old squeeze driving round the North Circular on the way to Sidcup Civic Centre, Brent Town Hall, the Gaumont State Theatre in Kilburn, or wherever it was taking place that year.

Once at the venue, the mums would all make camp across several rows of seats. This was our 'pit stop', where we would head to change costumes, grab a sandwich or, for the girls, to get a top-up of hairspray – you don't want a fringe flopping about while you're doing the sword dance. When I think back to those days, I still see and smell those great toxic clouds of spray hanging in the air. My mother loved it, even though it was a lot of work for her. They were an important social occasion for her and she delighted in watching the performances, chatting away to the other mums and giving out the recipes for her cakes. There would be few, if any, dads present though; like my father, they would be off playing or watching football or golf, or something.

I have such fond memories of those competitions. I often picked up a prize for my 'fling' or 'lilt'. All competitors got at least a certificate, either highly commended, commended or novice, then there were gold, silver and bronze medals for the different dance disciplines and a cup for overall winners. A panel of three judges watched your routine and several bagpipe-players would accompany you. It was quite a pressurised situation for a youngster to be in, but I was never nervous, because I was always ready for it. Kathleen and Melody prepared us well. The day would usually finish up around 6 p.m., when we would all pack up and go home. Our mother would be beaming with pride if we came away with a medal or a cup.

When we got home, my father might still be out at the pub with the lads from football. He didn't pay too much attention to our dancing, although he did help me take my big toenail off once with a pair of pliers. I found that you could get a much better 'pointe' position (standing on your toes) if you didn't have a big toenail. My father thought you could solve anything with Vaseline, Sellotape or a pair of pliers, and in this instance I agreed with him. I found that the pain barrier was worth it, if you got something out of it – like a better performance. And yes, it hurt like hell.

I would take the 'no pain no gain' theory to its limit later in my life. Whether I was endangering myself to make people laugh, or pushing myself to the limit to finish an order of pots on time, it didn't matter to me whether it hurt. I was single-minded in what I was doing, and I would do it come hell or high water. Of course, this would backfire sometimes, but I'm certain the discipline and stamina I needed to be a dancer helped me cope with the physical demands of running my own pottery.

* * *

When I opened my own pottery at Highgate in 1989, I was determined to base my business plan on the way Isaac Button had worked. It may sound strange, but I was truly inspired by his story. He was talented, unpretentious and phenomenally hard-working. The honesty in him and his work really appealed to me. He also liked a drink, as I do. It was said of him that he never left a pub the same day he entered it. I expect that, up on that lonely moor, there weren't many other ways to let off steam after working so hard. However, there was one thing about Isaac Button that I had somehow overlooked for a long time: he never made much money.

There's a Welsh saying that describes a job that is a lot of hard work for little reward. I won't trouble you with the original this time, but in English it goes: 'Like shearing a pig: lots of noise, but not much wool.' I don't know how Isaac Button would have put it; I suspect he never had the time to think about it. His wares had always been cheap and the villagers who bought them saw them as semi-disposable; the only way the country potters could make even a modest living was to make as many pots as they could, as quickly as they could. That is why he worked at the speed he did – he had no choice.

By 1965, when I was opening my eyes for the first time and no doubt bawling, and the Beatles were asking for 'Help!', Isaac Button was woefully out of touch with his market. He was still making cheap products, but his clientele was abandoning the countryside to go and work in the cities. He lived only another four years after retirement. Maybe that's not surprising, since he must have done the work of two men during his lifetime.

I did have a choice and I stand by it. For years I would diligently and doggedly follow in Isaac Button's footsteps until my body and bank balance finally rebelled in the 2000s. And to this day, I have never sheared a pig or tried to put a finger up a fly's arse. But I would never rule anything out.

3

BUILT LIKE A SPARROW

My forebears have always liked a good yarn. There are probably more myths and legends per square inch of Wales than anywhere else in the world. Believe it or not, the earliest known prose stories of the British Isles were written in Middle Welsh during the twelfth and thirteenth centuries. They were little known outside Wales until the mid-nineteenth century, when they were published in translation as *The Mabinogion* by an aristocratic

Englishwoman, Lady Charlotte Guest. These stories of ancient royal families, set in a magical Welsh landscape, inspired J.R.R. Tolkien and laid the foundations for the fantasy fiction genre so popular today.

Since they evolved before most people could read or write, they were originally passed down through word of mouth by storytellers, or bards. If I'd have been born a few hundred years earlier, I like to think I'd have made a good bard, telling tales for pints of ale, instead of throwing myself around tiny stages in dingy basements in the 1980s.

One of the best-known tales of the Mabinogion concerns Lleu Llaw Gyffes and Blodeuwedd, which I will summarise briefly for you. Ask me to pronounce these names for you some time, then we can both have a laugh. As a young man, Lleu's own dear mother placed a terrible curse on him, which meant he would never be able to take a human wife. This sort of thing was standard practice back then, but so too was magic and luckily for Lleu, his Uncle Gwydion, a renowned wizard, artfully side-stepped the curse by conjuring up a woman for Lleu made entirely of flowers: oak, broom, and meadowsweet, to be precise. Her name was Blodeuwedd, or 'Flower Face', and despite being entirely plant-based, she was indeed all woman.

Unfortunately, Lleu soon annoyed his flower-bride by leaving her alone for several days while he went off on an extended hunting trip with his pals. While taking a walk to think things through, Blodeuwedd clapped eyes on the true love of her life – not Lleu, but the dashing Gronw Pebr, Lord of nearby Penllyn. It was love at first sight, they had fallen deeply, and so, obviously, the first thing they decided to do was get rid of poor Lleu.

But people in these legends don't die easily and this was especially true in Lleu Llaw Gyffe's case. He could only perish at dusk alongside a riverbank, when wrapped in a net, and providing he had one foot placed on a steaming cauldron and the other on a goat, *and* with a spear that would take a whole year to make. What were the chances of that?

Blodeuwedd used all her flowery charms to wheedle this information out of her husband, and then informed her lover. You can only imagine the language out of Gronw when he was told what was required to kill his rival. But to give him his due, he did what was necessary, and a year later he and Blodeuwedd laid their fiendish trap. Everything was going to plan right up to the moment Gronw flung his custom-made spear; Lleu, precariously straddling a goat and a cauldron, was a sitting target. But he had wisely held something back from his flower maiden, and when it struck, he did not die, but instead turned into an eagle and soared away into the sky.

Still, with Lleu gone, Blodeuwedd and Gronw took control of his land. Uncle Gwydion was heartbroken, blaming himself for his nephew's plight. He searched all over Wales, high and low, braving the inevitable persistent drizzle. Finally, in a deep valley under Snowdon, he discovered a frail Lleu perched high in a tree, living off the maggots festering in his wound. Gwydion transformed him once more into a human and they returned home. Gronw and Blodeuwedd had fled, but they were hunted down. Gronw was simply run through, but old Uncle Gwydion had something more creative in mind for Blodeuwedd; at Llyn Morwynion, under his spell, she became an owl; forever the hated bird, the night-flyer and rodent killer.

What became of Lleu I do not know, but I doubt he allowed his uncle to do any further matchmaking. Maybe he returned to being an eagle. Now that wouldn't be a bad life. Or maybe he roamed the hills, alone and brooding, living the kind of life that the mountains made dreams about.

The Wales I remember as a boy was not exactly magical, but there was something in its landscapes that captivated me and fired my imagination. We always took our family holiday there, often staying at the atmospheric Baskerville Arms Hotel, just outside Hay-on-Wye. Looming above us were the Black Mountains, bleak and forbidding, usually shrouded in mist or engulfed by low cloud. We'd drive into the mountains and then walk to the top of peaks like Hay Bluff or Lord Hereford's Knob.

This was a land where I could invent my own myths and legends, where I was the hero. I would stare out of the car window, forehead pressed to the glass, and daydream about living on the mountainside, all alone, surviving off the land with nothing but my penknife; it would be all I needed to build a shelter, hunt for food or fight off my enemies.

Those dreams of mine, the idea of escaping somewhere solitary, became something of an obsession after I left primary school in 1976. Until then, life had been pretty much idyllic. I had lived my first ten years in a lovely protective bubble, screened from a harsh, unforgiving world by the safe, middle-class world my parents had constructed for me. I was lucky.

That summer was a scorcher, the hottest for over 350 years. I can remember having to fetch water in a bucket from a standpipe at the end of our road. Everywhere you went the grass was parched and brown. For a young lad without a care in the world, it was a wonderful time. We went to the Pembrokeshire coast on holiday and spent endless days sweltering on vast, shimmering sandy beaches. My father was great fun when we went away and acted like a big kid; everywhere else, he was in a constant bad mood.

When we arrived at the beach in the morning, he would plonk my sister and me down on the picnic rug, then haul us across the sand as fast as he could, a big gangly athlete sweating in the sun. He would only stop when my mother indicated where she thought we should sit. I would note the faces of other children looking on jealously, wishing their dads would do that for them. It made me strangely proud that he was so different and unconventional. It is a trait I have inherited from him. I have never worried about making a fool of myself for the sake of having fun.

As the dry spell dragged on into August, the situation became serious: reservoirs were running empty, crops were perishing and forest fires were raging. The government took the unprecedented step of appointing a Minister for Drought in the form of Denis Howell. It was a rare inspired move from Number 10, as a week later there was thunder and lightning, lashing rain storms, and then nationwide floods. The drought had broken. Denis Howell became known as the Minister for Floods.

The long, hot summer was over. And so was my childhood. That soaking, cold September, I started at St Mary's Church of England High School in Hendon and came face to face with the real world. It was bigger, nastier, smellier and scarier than anything you, I or indeed the Mabinogion bards could make up.

The stories I had been told about secondary school worried me, and I found myself really anxious for the first time in my life. I was not keen on having my head flushed down a toilet by a vicious, chain-smoking fifth-former. You have to remember, I was built like a sparrow at the time, and they could probably have flushed all of me down.

It might sound strange, looking at me now, but I was a late developer and in my first few years at St Mary's, I was constantly looking up at the world, dreading whoever was looking down at me. Older kids would come up and ask for my soap money; cash for the right to use soap in the toilets. I paid up. There was nothing you could do about it; certainly not tell anyone, as there was nothing worse than a snitch. It is strange how, even as a young boy, I understood this pathetic code of so-called honour.

The shock of my grisly secondary school reality pushed me further into my other fantasy world. Soon, I gave up the idea of living as a hermit in Wales and became obsessed instead with becoming a long-distance lorry driver. The idea of climbing up into the cab and being able to drive to a thousand faraway places enthralled me. I guess what I really wanted was to be as far away from St Mary's as possible. In a handful of months I had been transported from a cosy, colourful little place into this nightmare world that reeked of stale fags and disappointment. Five years in this place was a life sentence. A curse. Death by a spear that took a year to make while eating maggots.

The transition might have been easier if I had been a competent student, but I was far from that. I'd always struggled with reading and writing and by my last year at Frith Manor, I was acutely aware the rest of my class had left me trailing with regards to literacy. This perception was reinforced every time we were asked to read aloud. When it was my turn, the sniggers of my classmates hit me hard as I stuttered my way through a passage, and I developed an inferiority complex, which was exacerbated in the more hostile environment of St Mary's. Of course, I didn't know there was a reason why words and numbers were such a puzzle for me. It would be another year or so before I was diagnosed as being dyslexic. In the meantime, my 'problem' felt like another target on my back.

I was found wanting socially, too. I was not into football, unlike most other boys. I was into Mike Oldfield's *Tubular Bells*, and this was a beating-up offence, so I tried to keep it quiet. I was academically average and virtually invisible in all other respects, and I felt that all too keenly. Naturally, I fell in with the boys who were known as the 'doffos', or geeks. But even they called me 'Jones' instead of Keith – like in the army. I did make an impact on one person: Barry Bastard, the bully (not his real name). He was quick to establish me as his dogsbody, carrying his books around for him. He would let me know where his classes were and I would hand over the books he needed and take back the ones he did not. Again, there was little I could do but endure it.

Outside school there was my dancing, which I was still mad keen on. I was regularly rehearsing and competing and it took up most of my weekends. On Saturdays when I was not dancing, and seeing as I was now at 'big' school, my father decided it was high time I was properly introduced to the London Welsh football club. He was one of their best players, still an incredibly fit man, who turned out for them until he was forty-six. I would go along to watch matches with my grandfather, Pa, who was the club president (and had been for years). Saturday afternoon football was what the two of them lived for.

Home games were played at the hallowed Gunnersbury Park in west London. This great expanse would host around fifty football matches running simultaneously, in all weather. Each team would take their own goal net out and put it up before the game; you could not leave them up and expect them to be there the next day. Pa would stand on the touchline, sitting on his shooting stick with Ricky the corgi by his side. He was the critic by whom all performances were judged. You would never hear him swear; a tut from him for a missed tackle or goal was like a bullet for the player concerned, and if the team were not

29

performing it was a machine gun: *tut tut tut tut*. On hearing this, grown men would bow their heads, disgusted with themselves for disappointing the 'old man'.

In the middle of the park was an enormous shed with a corrugated roof, probably made of asbestos. This was the changing rooms and showers. Think of yourself in a place so steamy you can hardly see your hand in front of you. The steam smells of mud and sweat and it clings to your nostrils. The door opens and cold air momentarily blows the clouds apart, revealing a mass of pink-red-brown-yellow muddy men of all shapes and sizes, laughing and shouting and talking so loud it roars. Afterwards it was always the pub, where the smell of Double Diamond beer and Hai Karate aftershave was almost as overpowering. We would drive home and if I tried to speak, my father would tell me to be quiet; I guess it took some concentration, negotiating the North Circular Road on six or seven pints.

This was my induction into 1970s manhood and as a scrawny, sensitive boy it left an impression. As surely as we would holiday in Wales every year, I knew that one day I was destined to take the field at Gunnersbury Park. Unfortunately, however, dear old Pa would never get to see me there. Towards the end of my first year at St Mary's, I watched him fall down the stairs and land in a broken heap at the bottom. My grandparents were looking after me at the time, as my mother had taken Sarah to an important dance competition. Grandmother was on the phone to my mother when it happened.

'Oh, Grandfather has fallen down the stairs,' she said, her voice light, mildly surprised, as if she were expecting him to get up in a moment, grumble lightly and dust himself down.

He did not get up. I knew he wouldn't. I don't know how, but I knew, immediately, that he was dead. I ran out into the street.

I shouted and ran. It was the first, but not the last, time I would watch a family member take a tumble down the stairs, and it left its mark on me.

This isn't a misery memoir or a Gothic horror, so I won't go on. But seeing my Pa die did nothing to reassure me about how my life was going. I carried on, a little older and a lot less cheery. Things did pick up. Although I was small, I had excellent stamina – which was probably due to my years of dance training – and I discovered that I was better than most at swimming, running and, believe it or not, walking. I was even in the school walking team. You should have seen me, this slip of a thing, wiggling my skinny hips and gliding across the track.

It was in art class, though, where my life changed for the better. Mr Mortman, the art teacher, could have been a Shakespearean actor; he was stately, well-spoken, precise and rather camp. He would direct a class rather than teach it – often chaotically. I really liked him. He was the only teacher who showed any sensitivity at all towards his pupils.

One afternoon during the first term, I walked into class and saw on the benches waiting for us lumps of what looked like mud or putty wrapped in black polythene. Predictably, the boys at the back picked theirs up and started to slam them down on the bench. I heard nothing, I was already transfixed by what lay in front of me. Mr Mortman restored a semblance of order and then addressed us. I don't know any Shakespeare, but I'll never forget this speech.

'What you have before you … is clay.' He paused for dramatic effect. 'It's terracotta clay, to be precise. I want you all to make something out of it.'

Just looking at this lump of clay washed away all the anxiety I usually felt when asked to do anything in class. I still hadn't touched it, and hadn't even begun to think what I was going to do with it, but felt excited by the endless possibilities of this material. I could do … anything with it. Unwrapping the clay, I ran my hands across the slippery surface, feeling its density, its texture. It felt amazing, like I was holding my own imagination there in my hands. All my thoughts and energy were focused on this slab of clay. Everything else was a blur, unimportant.

I started by making a sphere, or should I say half a sphere, pushing the clay into the palms of my hands and gently smoothing it over with my finger. It felt right. Most of my classmates didn't feel the same; the back row boys quickly recognised that clay pellets were a rich source of ammunition. Within minutes, our white school shirts were all decorated with red terracotta blotches. Ignoring this carnage, I completed the other half of my sphere and stuck the two together. I was making an owl.

I started to inflict a surface technique on the clay using one of the wooden tools provided to dig into it and create a crude feather effect. I was completely lost in the process. It was while I was carrying out this 'technique' that Mr Mortman, distancing himself from the main bombardment, glided over to where I was busy working away with what appeared to be concentration. I was aware of him watching me and felt myself tense up.

'My, my, that looks very nice, Keith!' he said, enthusiastically. 'You may have something there. You seem to be quite talented at this. Well done. Carry on.'

A great clod of terracotta could have struck me straight between the eyes at that moment and I wouldn't have felt a thing; it was the first time anyone had praised me at St Mary's. Mr Mortman was possibly even more stunned than I was, not simply because he had a boy in his class doing something he had told him to do, but by the fact that he may have some real talent for it.

He produced a bottle and got us to pour its contents into plastic paint bowls. This, he explained, was liquid 'slip' and we could use it to decorate our work. I began to prepare mine, thinking how it might complement or even enhance what I had already made. Words in a book and on blackboards were not easy for me to penetrate and decode, but here was a discipline that seemed to come naturally to me. This clammy, malleable substance that had been dug out of the ground, together with the clear liquid in the bowl, were magic ingredients that I could understand. Here was something that intrigued and beguiled me, that had a hook in me, and I hadn't even been aware of it before coming to school that morning.

Mr Mortman, bless him, recognised my enthusiasm and indulged me. Within days I was allowed free rein in the art room. I started coming in during lunchtimes, after and even before school. It was a safe haven for me. Barry Bastard would never come looking for me in there, though there were reminders that I still had to be on my toes. Once, someone put razor blades in the clay and I 'found' them when kneading it into shape. The clay went pink, and so did my hands. Fortunately, the cuts were only superficial. The room was kept locked after that incident and I was given a key to access it.

I wanted to learn everything about pottery. I even read books, which was something I rarely did, and rarely do now, for that matter. Mr Mortman taught me what he knew; pottery was not really his forte, but he could centre a piece of clay. I found that so difficult, initially; it was like attempting clutch control on a car for the first time, you never think you will manage it properly even once, let alone master it. I almost stopped breathing, I was concentrating so hard on this one, seemingly simple task. But the clay would still fly off in all directions. So I practised hard and often.

The room had two wheels; one was a kick wheel and the other was electric and had a pedal that you put into teeth to keep it at a certain speed – I have one similar to this in my workshop now. Everything literally fell into place once I could centre, from the day I began to feel in control of that simple but devilishly difficult process. Once the clay was there, I had control and could work on 'getting it up'. Doing this correctly is about knowing where and when to apply small increments of pressure with your knuckle and fingers, while keeping the clay moist with water at the same time. You develop an instinct for it.

The art room became my playground. I was usually the only person in there, so I could do as I pleased. Progress was slow, but I was in no hurry. I do remember one big step forward. I had made a very large beaker, a fairly well-thrown one, I thought, nice and thin. I put a blue glaze on it, then I dipped it in a white glaze followed by a brown iron glaze and these all reacted together to create something I considered to be original. It wasn't, of course, but that didn't matter, I had 'discovered' the alchemy of ceramics; in my little pottery, my own little world, I was stumbling across new and exciting ways of doing things.

I owe much to Mr Mortman; he placed so much trust in me, he even gave me a crash course in electronics and showed me how to replace the element in the kiln. Now this was a 440 volt, 3 phase kiln – one mistake and I would have been vaporised! That would have been difficult to explain to the headmaster and my family, but then, times were different.

Another reason I felt drawn to pottery and loved being in the art room was because I felt in control there. I sensed very strongly in that first year that I had no influence over other aspects of my life. Increasingly, I felt I needed things around me to have order; I needed things 'just so' to feel comfortable in myself. Nowadays,

I recognise that this was Obsessional Compulsive Disorder (OCD), but back then I had never heard that term and knew nothing about it. It had always been there below the surface, but the stress of joining St Mary's, followed by Pa's shocking and sudden death, brought it to the fore. I found it increasingly difficult to make sense of the disorder going on around me. Pottery and its rules and processes, certainties and rituals, became my coping mechanism.

Two years on, in the third year (or Year 9 for the young folk out there), I was still struggling. My dyslexia had been diagnosed, but this actually put me back another step; it was one more thing to set me apart from the crowd, in a negative sense. And Barry Bastard was still making my life miserable. One day in a technical drawing class, he asked me to hand over his books and I decided, on the spot, that this had to stop. Now. I was still half his size, but out of sheer desperation I conjured up some strength, grabbed him by the throat and squeezed, hard. He started to go blue. Then he went bluer.

Eventually, someone pulled me off, I cannot remember who. There was some concern for me for a time after that, and I had to go and see a school counsellor during the lunch hour – for three months. She would ask me how I was feeling: 'Like I don't belong here,' I might well have answered. However, after this the bully left me alone. Like a large animal bitten by a smaller one, he steered clear, although he continued to pick on others.

I had to wait until I was fifteen to start growing physically. But then I more than made up for lost time, shooting up to well over six feet – six feet three inches, to be precise. Following my growth spurt, my father suddenly reckoned I had potential as a centre back for the London Welsh, so I was persuaded to go with him on the weekly pilgrimage to Gunnersbury Park. I had never been a fan of the game, but I could see it meant a lot to him, so I went and bought a pair of size-12 football boots.

I played in defence for the Fourth XI, braved the shower block and joined in the post-match inquests in the nearby Bell and Crown pub. I could only imagine what Pa would have made of me, though; he'd have been tut-tutting away on the touchline. It wasn't going to last, as a Saturday that revolved around football was never going to be my idea of a good time. I was no good at it, either. Grudgingly, my father conceded the point, and my brief football career was over.

I was glad, as I definitely had better things to do. Central London was just a 45-minute Tube ride, and I preferred to spend my weekends exploring what the city had to offer. I was struck by its contrasts. I loved the Docklands, at that time still a derelict wasteland. It reminded me of those desolate Black Mountains on our family holidays. Then there was the randomness and edge of places like Camden Market. In among the market stalls, with their rows of junk, second-hand records and musty hippy clothes, were characters right out of the bar scene in *Star Wars*. It was a coming together of intergalactic tribes: green-haired freaks, top-hatted giants in heels, and grizzled long-hairs infused with patchouli oil. All you got in Finchley were glowering skinheads.

One Saturday afternoon, as I was exiting the Tube at Camden Town Station, I spotted a poster for an exhibition at the Victoria and Albert Museum featuring the work of British studio potter Lucie Rie. I was stopped in my tracks by the image of this incredible bottle she had made, the most unusual, beautiful piece of pottery I had ever seen. In fact, I thought of little else from that moment until I was transfixed by the real thing the following week.

room, lumps of clay in my hands, they had nothing to do with me. What made them take notice, eventually, was my sudden and dramatic transformation from super-doffo geek into, of all things, a New Romantic. Remember them? Kilts and hairspray and all that. I bet you didn't see that coming!

I had never been that into music. Nothing had made me sit up and take notice until I bought the single 'One Step Beyond' by Madness in the autumn of 1979. I knew nothing about ska, or its Jamaican origins, but I knew this was something that made me want to dance. It was infectious. I became hooked, though not on Madness, as I quickly decided they were too mainstream for my tastes. What I craved was something more experimental.

I loved the weird sounds I was hearing on John Peel's Radio 1 show every night at 10 p.m. Bands like The Cure, Echo and the Bunnymen, Bauhaus, Southern Death Cult and Wasted Youth enticed me over to the darker side of the post-punk music scene. With hindsight, I suppose I was always drawn towards the unconventional; we *are* talking about a boy who danced and potted his way through adolescence, after all. For me, it seemed dull and a little lazy *not* to explore the alternative options, to accept blindly what was pushed across the table towards you.

The weekly music newspaper *Sounds* became my bible and every weekend I would go down to the Virgin Megastore on Oxford Street to seek out their latest recommendations. It followed that I started to take an interest in fashion; going into London, you would see these gothic punk types, in black leather and make-up, like vampire peacocks on the Tube. They took trouble over their appearance, and I thought they were magnificent.

Then one Sunday morning, sometime in May, I watched a TV documentary called *20th Century Box*, which was all about the Blitz Club and the burgeoning New Romantic scene. It featured a new group, Spandau Ballet, playing live at the Scala cinema. What I saw combined music with glamour, style and theatre and it captured my imagination, big time. It was also filmed in black and white, which added to its cool aesthetic. I was so captivated I took myself straight down to Camden Market and bought an outfit based on what I had seen. Oh yes, now I was definitely no longer the doffo ugly duckling.

With hindsight, my decision to go to the next house party to which I was invited, dressed in all my finery, was a brave one. That fateful night I wore tartan trousers, a white collarless evening shirt, a silk sash around my waist and suede pixie boots on my massive feet. As a finishing touch, I had a Palestinian keffiyeh scarf wrapped round my neck. Consider that image, if you dare. The party was in a really cool, art deco house and I have to say I was by far the most flamboyant-looking person there. The Hull brothers were impressed; they could not believe I was the same person who had been fiddling about with clay owls and the like since the first year. Nor could I, to be honest.

I hung out with them a lot over the next couple of years, but my New Romantic phase was short-lived. I got beaten up soon after, at another party, by some older blokes who took exception to my clothes. I remember the morning after, standing at a bus stop with a split lip and a black eye, and a kind old lady asked me if I was okay. I nodded miserably in reply, but thought to myself, Nah, I'm not into the scene enough to put up with this every weekend. Besides, Spandau Ballet had quickly turned out to be a rather shitty funk-soul band.

Now I was in with the Hull brothers, and it was an edgy kind of fun hanging out at their house. It was a great, boisterous hub with people constantly coming and going, all presided over chaotically by their mother, who cared not what went on under her roof, so long as there was one. It was the polar opposite to life with my parents at Walmington Fold, which is probably why I spent so much time there. West Finchley was safe, suburban and white, whereas Neasden, where the Hulls lived, was a different world – a vibrant, multicultural one with a hint of danger around every corner.

It was my first exposure to the true diversity of London. Their friends and neighbours were from all corners of the world, living together in a community that was ten times more exciting than where I came from, and which was only a seven-mile cycle ride away. Seeing where they lived, I realised exactly why Steven and Sean were more streetwise than I was. What endeared me to them, I think, was my willingness to put myself through the pain barrier to get a laugh.

The first daft thing I can remember doing was letting them spray paint around my outline on their bedroom wall. I held the pose while they let fly with the aerosol cans, pissing themselves laughing. It was an excruciating business scrubbing the paint off my skin afterwards, but it gained me some kudos and I played up to that zany, risk-taking reputation for many years afterwards.

Music-wise, Steven and Sean were into soul, but their cousin Anthony was a bit of a punk and into the same bands that I was, so we started going to gigs together. I was so lucky to be a teenager in London in the early 1980s. You could go and see a great band every night of the week and it was peanuts to get in, even at the bigger venues. The first bigger venue we went to was the Rainbow Theatre in Finsbury Park, a massive art deco structure that held 3,000 people. It felt like I was entering a cathedral that night, which is quite fitting, as it is now an Evangelical church.

The headliners were Classix Nouveaux, but we went to see

the main support act, Theatre of Hate. I had been a fan ever since hearing their first single, 'Original Sin' – a song that, to this day, makes the hairs stand up on the back of my neck. They were an inspiration playing live, raw and electrifying. Watching them was like being plugged into the National Grid. The date was 11 April 1981, the ticket cost £3.50 and the night was a watershed moment for me.

I asked for a guitar for my sixteenth birthday and got one. It was only an acoustic, but I was determined to learn how to play, so I could join a band and perhaps be onstage at the Rainbow myself one day. I took some lessons, mastered some basic chords, then bought a cheap electric guitar. We even got a band going, which we rehearsed in the Hulls' bedroom. One of their girl-friends sang. Like everything else that went on there, it was somewhat chaotic, and with the Hulls not really that interested, it fizzled out. I stalled in trying to master the guitar, although I did start writing songs on it. Fairly simple songs. I thought perhaps they would come in handy somewhere down the line.

*   *   *

So there I was, still sitting opposite the careers advisor. She was running out of pamphlets to flap at me and was getting flustered. I felt sorry for her. Surely she never dreamed of one day sitting here while some upstart ignored her helpful suggestions. Her hand briefly hovered over 'Join the Gas Board', then she thought better of it and put the ball in my court.

'All right, Jones. What *do* you want to do?'

I took the plunge. I had to.

'I want to be a potter.'

For the first time, the careers advisor smiled. Then she chuckled.

'Oh well, I'm afraid you're on your own there,' she said, and promptly dismissed me.

It was a hopeless waste of time, as I suspect most of her interviews were, but she was right in a way. I would spend much of the next twenty years on my own ... hunched over a potter's wheel.

That summer I got the five 'O' levels required to go on to study 'A' levels. 'O' stood for 'ordinary', not the greatest motivator. 'A' stood for 'advanced', so at least that hinted at some sort of achievement. Despite still hating St Mary's, I felt that with my unlimited access to the art room, it would be as good a place as any to continue my studies. Besides, I got to choose my best subjects: Art, Graphics and Design, and Technology. I had a vague idea that I might go on to art college at Harrow or Camberwell, which both had good reputations for ceramics.

As it turned out, those two years in the sixth form were truly formative; the decisions I made and the friends I met during that time hugely influenced the direction my life would take. So did my explorations around my city. Everything any young, curious, open-minded young man could ever wish for was right there on the doorstep. The times I remember most fondly were the weekdays I spent exploring London on my own. I was supposed to be in school, but I would leave after registration and head for Hendon Central and catch the Tube into town. I felt totally free; no one knew where I was or what I was doing.

My favourite London view is still the one you get standing on Waterloo Bridge, looking in either direction. That, for me, is the heart of the city, with all the arteries reaching out north, east, south and west. It sends shivers down my spine. From there I would take the short walk to the Royal Festival Hall. It's a real Marmite building – you either love it or you hate it, and I love it. It is a brilliantly conceived, wide-open indoor space for visitors to hang out in. It also houses my favourite carpet in all the world, the classic net and ball design by Peter Moro, who was also one of the building's architects. Maybe reading this you get an idea why I took these day trips alone: imagine the reaction of a mate when I suggested we go to the South Bank to check out the fabulous carpet!

The place where I spent the most time was the Victoria and Albert Museum. I could easily spend the whole day wandering round the galleries; something different would catch my eye, some German salt-glazed bottles, or a contemporary Bernard Leach studio pot, and then I would sit myself down with my pencil and pad and sketch them. It was an education in itself and opened my eyes to all the possibilities of ceramics, the different styles and techniques, what clay was used to create them, and what glazes.

All my bunking off and gallivanting around town cost money, though, and after a while my parents suggested it was time I found myself a part-time job. So a few weeks later I found myself employed as a junior shelf stacker at the Whetstone branch of Tesco. I would work Thursday and Friday evenings and all day Saturday for £1 an hour.

I was immediately taken under the wing of someone who had gone to my primary school, Frith Manor. Anthony had been in the year below me there, quiet and angelic. Now he was a scruffy, scary long-haired biker type, although at this stage without the bike. He was saving up for one, he said, but it would take a bloody long time as he was the Tesco 'YTS' boy. This meant he was on a government 'youth training scheme', which was more like a government 'youth slave labour scheme', as he took home about £27 for a full working week. Suffice to say, his heart was not in it. Which meant we were going to have some fun.

Anthony and I shared the same warped sense of mischief, and for a year or so we wrought havoc in aisle number one, where it was our responsibility to keep the shelves fully stocked. We were back and forth constantly with boxes of tinned vegetables, flour, sultanas, tea, or whatever was running out, making sure there were never any gaps. That was a supermarket cardinal rule – no gaps.

In time, we became highly skilled at filling all kinds of gaps, in all kinds of random, novel ways. Biscuit gaps were our favourite, as biscuit packets were the most satisfying, crumbly kind of thing to kung-fu kick into place. Customers would pass by openmouthed as I was head-butting a packet of chocolate digestives into a gap that, strictly speaking, was not there. It amazed me that nobody ever said anything, or complained.

Every Saturday there would be an announcement over the tannoy system: 'Could Mr Jones please go to the front of the shop, you have a visitor.' It would be my aunt, Brenda, with my weekly allowance. My aunt had no children, was divorced and had a well-paid job with the Midland Bank. My sister and I got £40 a week from her, each, which was a very decent amount in 1982. She would pop in and hand it to me in a little envelope with the date, amount and running total for the year. Add that to my wages, and I was very nicely off. I could now afford to take cabs home from parties, and even opened an account with Medway Taxis in Highgate. Not bad for a young lad still at school.

As far as I was concerned, most of the other staff at Tesco were to be avoided, especially Mick, the weekend butcher's assistant, in his bloodstained white coat that reeked of offal and mince fat.

But Mick lived near Anthony, and somehow, against my better judgement, we fell into the habit of walking home together. Underneath the offal stains, I discovered Mick was a bit of a dandy and a right old music buff. He was also a big Theatre of Hate fan, and somewhat annoyingly had seen them more times than I had.

I pricked up my ears when I heard he was in a band himself. They were called the Obvious Wigs and had actually played two gigs up to this point. Mick was their guitarist and main songwriter. Impressive as this news was, it was all conveyed in a very understated way as Mick had a habit of speaking almost under his breath, so you sometimes had to strain to catch what he was saying. One evening as we ambled down Totteridge Lane, Mick intoned that the band's singer, Shag McGurk, had hung up his microphone. They were on the hunt for a new front man.

'I could be your singer!' I blurted, without thinking.

'Really?' whispered Mick. 'What are you doing next Tuesday?'

★   ★   ★

According to Mick's meticulously accurate band diary, my audition took place in the dining room at his mum and dad's house during autumn half term 1982. The other two band members were schoolmates of his from Finchley Catholic High School: Dean or 'Dong' on drums and Nigel on bass. The latter was the nephew of Phil Mogg of legendary 1970s rock band UFO, so I thought the band had a hint of real rock pedigree.

The big question was, could I sing? I had no idea. And the sad answer when I tried was no, not really. I had written a few songs in my bedroom, but had never sung in front of anyone, ever, until now. We ran through one of Mick's songs with me doing my best impression of Pete Murphy, the lead singer of Bauhaus.

The deep gothic drawl did not suit the song. At all. 'Dong' didn't hide the fact that he thought I was laughable. When he finished sniggering, I had another go and decided to concentrate on trying to sing in tune, which I discovered I could do. Mick and Nigel must have seen something they liked, because they gave me the nod. I was now an Obvious Wig.

Our first gig was in January 1983 at the Finchley Catholic High School sixth-form common room. Mick only just got back in time from Stratford-upon-Avon, where he had been to see *King Lear* with his English class. Okay, these were not high-cred origins, but after playing our energetic set to a select audience, we held court in the Swan and Pyramids pub and I felt something had changed in me; I felt like a lead singer. Inwardly, I was still full of self-doubt, but stick me in front of a crowd and I knew I could sweep that to the back of my mind and put on a show.

You could never have called us a punk band, but our roots were undeniably in the do-it-yourself ethos the original move-ment was all about. None of us were musically talented, but we made up for it with enthusiasm, creativity and attitude. Our songs were fast and direct and Mick's lyrics were strong, heavily influenced by Paul Weller, George Orwell and the odd charac-ters that lurked in the warehouse at Tesco.

With no manager or contacts we knew a proper venue would never book us, so we had to generate our own gigs and build a fanbase. The first one we set up was at Old Finchleians Football Club, only half a mile from my house. We made posters, photocopied them and handed them out at school, parties, everywhere. We sweated on the days leading up to the gig, doubting whether anyone would turn up. This was a feeling I was going to become very used to. On the night, a couple of our mates' dads sat on the door taking £2 off everyone and to our astonishment the cash began to pile up.

By the time we took the stage the place was rocking, with about 300 kids packed in and dancing along to us. It was the first time I got that buzz you get from a crowd who are noisily appreciating what you are doing onstage; one of the best feelings ever. We even played one of my songs, 'Julia', a sensitive little ditty about unrequited love, on which I also played guitar.

A friend of mine, Alec, came all the way from Crouch End to see us. He was the drummer in a band called the Stingrays, who made records and played proper gigs. He said we were great and that we might be able to support them sometime. The atmosphere in the dressing room – or rather the club house kitchen – after the gig was electric, and we were ecstatic. It was our first inkling that this music thing might go further than our local football club.

My last clear recollection of that night is more down to earth, however. My friend Bonnie found his crash helmet full of lager-puke at the end of the evening. And no, it wasn't me. Bonnie was a real stoner and too far gone to be riding his moped home, but no one was going to stop him. We watched, mouths open, as he carefully tipped the vomit out, and then put the helmet on. There were still bits dripping down his face as he turned to bid us farewell.

'Bye guys. Great gig!' he slurred, before tottering off for the ride home.

I think the reason that night stands out is because it so captures the essence of those days: the fun, the laughter and the silliness. We had no responsibility but to ourselves. They really were golden times.

I left school that summer. I passed my three 'A' levels, but decided against going to college. I resolved to find a job at a pottery workshop instead. But not straight away. I spent what was to be my last summer of youthful freedom working for Lieutenant-Colonel Stanley Williams, the father of my dancing teacher. He owned a number of large houses in Highgate and one of them was always in need of some light repairs or a lick of paint. He paid quite well – cash in hand – so I had plenty to spend on clothes, records, gigs, beer and taxis.

The Obvious Wigs played a second gig at Old Finchleians, but it was not a triumphant return. There were fewer people, a terrible onstage sound and we played like a box of turds. Afterwards, instead of celebrations, laughter and puking in crash helmets, there was a lively and frank discussion about the performance, which ended with Dong quitting the band and storming off. He stormed back again briefly for a couple of rehearsals but then left for good, citing my voice and, of course, musical differences as his reasons for leaving.

With my career as a rock star seemingly stalled and my parents' once polite enquiries about my future now reaching the level of 'nagging', I realised it was time to bite the bullet.

I placed an advert in *Ceramic Review*. It was brief and to the point: *Young, enthusiastic eighteen-year-old seeks apprenticeship in a pottery. Please call 01-346 3098.*

I thought it would at least keep them off my back for a while, although I was not hugely confident of getting a response. I waited and waited. A little over two weeks later, I answered the phone and heard a gruff voice, straight off a building site, shouting at me.

'Oi, is that Keith?' it hollered.

'Yes. This is Keith.'

'I heard you wanted to do some pottery.'

My jaw dropped. He said his name was Robert Hudson from Harefield Pottery. As he spoke, I wondered if he looked as angry as he sounded. Maybe he was permanently incandescent with rage. I was not sure I wanted to 'do' pottery with him. I had imagined working for a nice, softly spoken, middle-class lady in a smock and a headscarf.

'Right,' Robert barked at me. 'Come out to Harefield, it's near Watford. In the middle of nowhere. Come next Friday and I'll give you an interview.'

And with that he rang off. I grabbed our London A–Z and scoured it for this Harefield place I had never heard of. It was about twenty miles away, in the borough of Hillingdon.

My mother gave me a lift that Friday, as I had worked out it would take more than two hours on public transport. Harefield Pottery was next to a canal. Adjacent was a quarry and a lonely cluster of business units, a plastic injection-moulding firm, a garage specialising in respraying, and a fibre glass pipe-making company.

I would like to say I felt as if I was stepping through time, back to the heyday of the industrial revolution, when these waterways were the major arterial routes, with countless barges heading back and forth, laden with goods, bound for Birmingham, Manchester, and beyond. But I was just shit scared of meeting Robert.

I walked into the yard, the knot in my stomach tightening. My first impression was that it was a real working pottery, something I had never seen on this scale before. There was a piece of machinery I recognised as a filter press. It was massive and would take ages to unload. I walked past it and into the pottery workshop, which contained several kilns and another, smaller, filter press. There were no potters to be seen, though, so I went back outside. It was eerily quiet.

'Is that you, Keith?'

I recognised the raspy tones, but could see nobody. Then I noticed two legs poking out from under a car. It was jacked up and Robert was underneath, tinkering with the engine. Obviously, I expected him to slide out and greet me properly, then show me round the place before taking me into an office for the interview. Maybe he would want to see what I could do on the wheel as well. I was prepared for that.

But Robert did not emerge from under the car. He asked another question instead.

'Can you shovel clay?'

'Yes, I think I can do that,' I replied. I was not really dressed for digging.

'What are you like at making tea?'

'Okay, I suppose.'

'You'd better not be late,' he added, with more than a hint of intimidation.

'No. I won't,' I said in a puny voice.

'All right. Come back on Monday morning at eight.'

Throughout this, Robert had continued working under the car. Realising the interview was over, I turned and walked slowly back to where my mother was parked.

'How did it go?' she asked, as I climbed in beside her.

It was a good question. The truthful answer would have been: 'I'm not sure.' But I couldn't say that, could I? I couldn't tell her I hadn't the faintest idea what my new boss even looked like, but I was certain he was some kind of nutter. It might upset her.

'Really well,' I answered, forcing a smile. 'I start on Monday.'

5
LEATHER, SWEAT AND BOOZE

Looking back now at 'my 1984' is like passing through a provincial railway station in an InterCity 125 at about a thousand miles an hour: I can almost feel the blast in my face as a great seething mass of people, places and memories whizz into me from the past. You could say it was one the first steps of two very different, but truly amazing journeys: by day, I was learning how to be a real potter, and by night, I was trying to become a rock star. Life was a buzz and pretty full-on.

Here is a taste of how I spent a typical day during the summer of 1984. Think the miners' strike, think record unemployment, think hair gel. Think the Wigs' tour! I was nineteen. Oh, to have that energy – and waistline – once more.

Thursday 14 June

05:00: Get up. Get dressed.

05:20: Walk a mile up to North Finchley. Catch the 13 bus.

06:00: Get off at Baker Street. Walk to Marylebone Station.

06:27: Catch train to Rickmansworth.

06:50: Arrive at Rickmansworth Station. Walk two miles along canal to Harefield Pottery.

07:30: Start work. My first job is to unload clay from our two filter presses. The one inside our workshop is a quarter of a ton and the one in the yard, a massive ton and a half.

These great metal hulks separate liquid and solids using pressure filtration, and so mix the clay and make it workable. A slip – a water and clay mixture – is pumped into the press and dewatered under pressure, allowing the clay to dry out on its thick, cast-iron filter plates. Lying on these plates is a layer of silk, a filter that catches the clay particles as the slip is pumped in. The water that is drained off through the silk pours out the bottom of the press and is clear as a mountain stream.

Opening the press is an effort; so is pulling apart the heavy filter plates and removing the clay cakes. There are thirty plates in the outdoor press, each weighing 200 kilos, and the clay cakes are 3 feet square, dense and heavy. Mercifully, the press in the workshop only has fifteen plates and the clay cakes are half the size.

Once all the clay is removed, I clean down the silk screens, push the plates back up and bolt them all together. I have to pay close attention now, because if the bolts are loose, or if there is snag in the silk screens, as soon as the pump is turned on again the slip will gush out and spray all over the workshop. Mopping up the mess is a time-consuming pain in the arse and this happens not infrequently during my first year at Harefield.

08.30: Robert and Alan arrive. My mantra is: 'My sole purpose is to keep in them in workable clay throughout the day … and make the tea.'

08:35: Make tea. Have my first Mars Bar of the day.

09:00: Now it's blunger time as I have to mix some clay. Sounds rude, but it isn't. The blunger is basically a giant mixing bowl. It is always full from the night before, so first I have to pump out the contents and sieve them into enormous barrels standing next to the filter press. From these, the mixture will be pumped into the press at the end of the day, ready for the process to begin all over again the next morning. To refill the blunger, I thoroughly mix together water and clay in huge, 30 kilo clay hop bins, then lift up the bins and empty the blend in. It takes five bins to fill up our blunger and I will repeat this process three times a day.

10:20: Make tea. Have a Mars Bar.

10:40: Start balling up clay for whatever Alan and Robert are making today. Most probably it will be bonsai pots or pot covers, so I will make up between two and five hundred balls of clay.

12:10: Make tea. Have a Mars Bar and think about this evening's gig at the Clarendon in Hammersmith. Robert and Alan will let me leave early as long as I finish my jobs first. After Dong had left, the Obvious Wigs had been without a drummer for six months. We had plenty of interest for the vacant spot and Mick, Nigel and I were frequently arranging auditions; some applicants even bothered to turned up, but no one fitted the bill.

At the very least when a drummer turns up to try out for your band, you expect them to have: a) a drum kit or b) their own transport. You'd think it pointless to arrive with neither, but more than one hopeful turned up with nothing more than a pair of drum sticks. The situation became so desperate we were forced to put our hands in our pockets and pay for a proper advert in *Melody Maker.* We got one reply. Expectations were low when the prospective new member, Glenn Morton, told us he came from Enfield and nobody remotely cool ever came from that place. But … he had a car … he had drums. And boy could he play them. He was in!

After that, things started to happen for us. We latched on to the trash/garage/psychobilly scene, more or less through my friendship with Alec from the Stingrays, one of the genre's key bands. The Wigs' music was not typical of the scene, but our noisy, rudimentary approach and Alec's patronage granted us membership to this select club; one that met exclusively in dank, smoky, subterranean cesspits. One of them being the Clarendon.

This week in June, we have three gigs booked. Three in a week! It is a landmark in our eyes, constituting the first

Wigs' 'tour', even though the gigs are all within a five-mile radius in central London. To mark the event, I design the 'Wigs' Tour 1984' mug, a must for every fledgling, tea-drinking rock 'n' roller. I make one for each band member and a few extra, for my sister Sarah and our roadie Steve Hart, who remains the proud owner of the mug in the picture.

12:15: Next is pugging (turning) clay and bagging it up into 25-kilo bags that we sell to schools, colleges and pottery suppliers. We have a large de-airing pugmill that will turn out – when used correctly – a ton of clay in an hour. I am getting the hang of it, standing on a platform to feed in the 15-kilo clay cakes. This gives me a good appetite for …

13:30: Lunchtime. Robert and Alan are both foodies and love rustling up something proper to eat. Sometimes, one of them will catch a fish from the canal and that will be our lunch. During the winter, most days they will stick a pan on top of the wood burner and throw in eggs, wild mushrooms and mouth-watering potatoes, fresh from Robert's vegetable patch.

13:50: After lunch there are any number of things I might have to do: load the kilns; glaze hundreds of bonsai pots; unload the filter presses, again; sweep the floors. This afternoon, I am making glazes. Glazes are cooked up from recipes, and the ingredients are a combination of minerals mixed together to produce a glaze that seals the ceramic surface and makes it waterproof.

Individual minerals have their own melting point when introduced to heat, and when they are mixed together they react with one another and create a new melting point. This is called a eutectic mixture. Cornish stone, for example, is a low-iron feldspar material primarily used as a flux in clay bodies and glazes. It melts at 1150–1800°C. China clay has a higher melting point, at 1700–1800°C. Mix the two together, in the right quantities, and you lower the melting point of the china clay and increase that of the Cornish stone.

Depending on what sort of finish you are aiming for, you then add other minerals to the recipe. For example, if I wanted a pale-green finish, the recipe would be as follows: Cornish Stone 41%, China Clay 12.5%, Flint 15.5%, Whiting 16.5%, French Talc 14%, Yellow Ochre 1.25%, Cobalt Carbonate 0.25%.

We mix our glazes at Harefield in quantities of 25 kilos and each step has to be carried out precisely. To begin, I weigh out the ingredients, add gallons of water, then blend them together in the industrial mixer. Next, the mix has to be sieved through a fine mesh, not once but twice. In one hand I hold a heavy jug to pour the mixture, and in the other a brush to swish back and forth, forcing every drop of the viscous mixture through the mesh. Once I have repeated this, my arm is ready to fall off. I can barely manage to switch the kettle on.

15:40: Make tea. Have two Mars Bars.

15:45: Help Robert finishing packing the large oil kiln with bonsai pots and pot covers.

16:15: Apply a batt wash to the kiln shelves. This is a liquid applied to the kiln shelves/bats to ensure pots don't stick together when they are being fired. (I make up my own mixture these days from 50% china clay, 50% alumina hydrate.)

16:30: Finish work. Brisk walk back along the canal to catch train into London. Eat another Mars Bar. Think about the day. I am a willing dogsbody, honing the tasks of my daily routine through trial and error, conscious that any mistake means repeating a task, getting behind and slowing down Alan and Robert. Day by day, even minute by minute, I devise new ways to increase my efficiency and get more done, more quickly. The demands, physically and mentally, are constant. To some extent, enthusiasm carries me through, but all those years spent performing the Highland fling have provided me with the stamina to cope with it all; each duty performed is a new dance to be rehearsed and perfected.

17:20: Arrive at the Clarendon, which is actually two venues: the larger Clarendon Ballroom upstairs, known as 'Klub Foot', home to London's psychobilly scene; and the more intimate basement bar, where we are playing tonight. In truth, the venue is extremely 'unwell' with its low, creaking stage, worryingly sticky floor, and bogs that would make a dung-shoveller retch. But we love it, and with a decent crowd in and distorted music blasting out of the decrepit PA, there are few places we would rather be of an evening.

17:30: We do our sound check. Tonight we are supporting a band called the Riff Gypsies, who none of us have heard of. They look and sound like one of the glam-punk bands that are cropping up, the most famous being Hanoi Rocks. We wonder what size crowd they will pull. We know what ours will be: ten of our mates and my father.

18:00: While we wait to go on, we take a seat in the bar upstairs. Being a Thursday and with no gig on upstairs, there are not many punters about. Outside, a desiccated, stroppy old lady is arguing with the bouncer, a Great Wall of China named Pete. Wearing a nightie under her filthy coat, she insists on being allowed back in – you have to be low down in life's pecking order to be banned from this place. Pete turns his back for a moment and the lady slips past and orders a drink. The barman refuses her.

As Pete bears down, this feisty one decides to make a stand; her very own dirty protest. Quick as a flash, she squats down and relieves herself. We furtively sip our pints as this unexpected floor show is played out. What she passes is bright purple, pure methylated spirit. There is not much Pete can do. He lets her finish her business and escorts her out.

20:30: The Wigs take the stage. There are eight people in the audience. Our bastard mates and my father have blown us out. Bloody Thursday gigs. Who needs them?

22:30: The gig is over. The Riff Gypsies play to fifteen people, including us. They are terrible. So were we, but there will be other nights here, better ones. Over the next two years this will become a home-from-home, albeit a seedy one that reeks of leather, sweat and booze. Within five years it will be bulldozed to make way for a new Tube station and shopping centre.

23:10: Help the band load the equipment into Nigel's Ford Zodiac and Glenn's Rover, then say my goodbyes and head for the station.

23:15: Get on the Tube at Hammersmith Broadway.

00:30: Arrive at West Finchley Station.

00:45: Arrive home. Make tea.

01:00: Have a shower. Looking forward to the weekend when the band are recording a demo at Pathway studios. Exciting. The Damned recorded their first album there, including 'New Rose', the first ever punk single. Other bands that have squeezed into the legendary cupboard-sized studio to record include: er ... Squeeze, Madness, The Police, Siouxsie and the Banshees, Elvis Costello, Sham 69, Dire Straits ... I keep on counting until I fall asleep.

05:00: Get up, do it all again and love every minute.

6

AS GREEN AS THE FIRST LEAF ON A SAPLING TREE

Have you ever met a lion? I have. They're big.

One broiling Sunday morning in the summer of 1987, my girlfriend Jo and I were racking our brains trying to think what we could do with our precious day of rest. It was shortly after breakfast and the heat haze was already distorting the view of the city down the hill from Archway Road. It would be a good day to get out of London.

'Hey, let's go to Windsor Safari Park! It'll be fun!' I blurted like an eight-year-old. She looked doubtful. 'It's not far; we could be there in an hour, take in the wildlife and then find a nice riverside pub for lunch.'

My enthusiasm won Jo over, so we jumped into my trusty red Ford Escort Estate and set off. I hadn't been to a safari park since primary school and was pretty damn excited at the prospect of driving through the animal enclosures. Yes, we were simple folk back then. By the time we arrived, the temperature was in the eighties and there was a sizable queue to get in. Inevitably, as we were inching our way forward, I cursed myself for being so British and having the same idea as everyone else simply because it was hot. At this rate, we'd have to change our lunch into after-noon tea – or dinner, even. We pressed on, wishing the car had air-conditioning.

Eventually we got into the park, and it was great. We laughed at the monkeys' antics as they gurned at us through the windscreen and gave thanks that they didn't make off with the wind-screen wipers. We spotted some wolves a long way off, under some trees, dozing, and some antelope swishing flies with their tails. Most of the animals were taking the heat in their stride, by staying asleep. By the time we got to the lion enclosure, it was getting towards lunchtime and sure enough, the wardens were throwing out great hunks of meat off the back of a truck – feeding time! All that was missing was a David Attenborough voiceover.

The snake of cars ground to a halt. The people in front of us, nearest to the lion action, were obviously engrossed. I felt a bit disappointed. The lions were a hundred metres away, and frankly, it wasn't much of a spectacle. I'd expected to see them closer up than this. It was a bit like being in a jam on the M25, even down to the man in the car behind picking his nose and shouting at his kids. Sweat began to trickle down my back. We were sweltering, but for obvious reasons, the windows had to be kept closed. Jo frowned and yawned. I started looking around for something to kid her about.

'Oh, look,' I said, pointing. 'Those lions are having a bit of a squabble.'

Three of them had broken away from the main feasting pack and had come together, roaring and flinging their massive paws about. We decided it was probably a dispute over a choice cut. It then occurred to me that *I* was a choice cut, in a lion's eyes. I put that thought out of my head and checked all the doors were locked. When I looked up, the three lions involved in the fracas seemed to be closer to us, and their attention was totally captivated by something, seemingly, behind our car.

'I swear they're looking at us,' I said, following this statement with a chuckle meant to comfort Jo, but which sounded decidedly nervous, even to my own ears.

I could see Jo's bottom lip starting to wobble as the lions broke into a slow trot and then a lope. My lip joined in. They were definitely coming our way. Quickly.

Now, would you say three adult lions would weigh about 750kg, roughly the same as my car? And they were running towards us at about 30 miles an hour. I acted quickly, lurching the car forward as far as I could to leave a bigger space for them to pass behind us. Surely they were only eager to cross the road? Surely.

'We're safe in here,' I squeaked, as we both automatically assumed the aeroplane 'brace' position. The flight safety voiceover is always so calm, don't you think? This was not calm.

Moments later, we felt the first impact as my driver's-side door crumpled inwards. The noise was huge. The second lion crashed onto the bonnet. I took a quick look up and saw him peering into the car, and his head almost filled the windscreen. The third rascal almost took my hatchback off – it was a miracle no glass was broken. We stayed down for an extra few seconds, panting, then slowly raised our heads. As we peeped over the dashboard, we saw the occupants of the other cars doing exactly the same – only their cars were untouched. Mine must have been shunted ten feet off the road. I was worried it would be a write-off. But mostly I was worried it wouldn't start. I turned the key.

To our eternal relief, the engine turned over. With shaking hands and a stupid grin on my face, I did the British thing and politely rejoined the queuing cars. As far as the lions were concerned, we were yesterday's news; they ambled off to finish their lunch and chew over the pathetic human cowering behind his steering wheel when they'd only nipped over to say 'hello'.

Jo and I completed the circuit of the park in a rather subdued manner. Basically, we were in shock. At the gate, I pointed out the damage to one of the park wardens.

'See what your prize exhibits have done to my car?'

'What do you want me to do,' he replied with a smirk, 'Tell 'em off?'

I got the distinct impression he'd used that line before.

If something like that happened these days, it would go viral before you even got home, but back then, with few witnesses, I wondered whether anyone would believe me when I told them what had happened. I drove home anticipating the terrible piss-taking I would get on Monday morning from Alan and Robert when I turned up at Harefield Pottery. They didn't need much of an excuse, of course, but this was a beauty. That wasn't the only reason I didn't want them to see the car in this state.

You see, it was down to them that I got it in the first place. The car represented a landmark in our relationship, and I feared that this accident might spoil that somehow.

*   *   *

I never had a huge desire to learn to drive when I was a teen-ager. Growing up in London, you didn't need a car as public transport could take you anywhere you wanted to go. And if it was late, and you had a Saturday job as well as an Auntie Brenda, you took a taxi. Despite this, as soon as I turned seventeen I started taking lessons, as it seemed to be the thing to do. Like everyone else in the early 1980s, the car I learned to drive in was an Austin 'Mini' Metro, which was one of the worst cars ever made. Personally, I'm a sucker for classic design, and this car was the opposite: a box on wheels, and a horrible, unreliable box at that.

As I crunched the gears, I preferred to imagine myself behind the wheel of an old Bristol 405, which was my dream car. Those luxury British saloons were made by the Bristol Aeroplane Company in the 1950s using the highest standard of craftsman-ship. They were all about style and built like tanks. I loved them. I'd like to see a lion try to butt one of those off the road. After a few lessons, I parked the idea of learning to drive and turned my thoughts to design instead; pottery, cars – it all came down to craftsmanship.

In the early years of motoring, the thought of a car being aesthetically pleasing did not occur to anyone in the industry. Cars were functional and clunky-looking, designed by engin-eers who were simply making something to take you from A to B. All that was changed by an American called Harley Earl, perhaps the most influential and innovative car designer of all time. From the very start of his career, his goal was to produce cars that were desirable and beautiful to look at, and he did exactly that, replacing the clunky boxes with seductive curves and streamlined bodies.

He made his name building outrageous one-off cars for silent-era Hollywood movie stars. The one he made for cowboy Tom Mix even had a leather saddle on its roof. He subsequently became head of design at General Motors, where his influence lit up the mass-produced car industry in the 1920s, with every other company replicating his methods. As he got older, his designs grew ever more ambitious; he was the man responsible for the futuristic Chevrolets, Buicks and Cadillacs with their great long tail fins. The fins served no purpose – they just looked amazing.

My real interest in Earl, however, was not in the cars he built, but rather his pioneering use of clay as a design technique. Before building a car, he would first make a full-sized model of it. So, for example, if the shape of the bonnet was not to his liking, all he had to do was add some clay or scrape some off. This process was quicker and cheaper than using sheet metal and wood, as other manufacturers had done before Earl came along, as it allowed the designer to visualise profiles and create them, immediately.

Like all truly great innovations, its genius is in its simplicity. And it is such a great idea that no one has come up with a better way to design cars ever since. The car that you drive will have been carved out of clay (or industrial plasticine as the substance now used is called) long before it was ever put into production. Working from sketches, car manufacturers employ a team of modellers who first make a one-third scale model of the car, before constructing a full-size one.

It's not solid, of course. A skeleton made of foam, plywood and aluminium is covered with a layer of warm plasticine 6–8 centimetres thick. The model can then be tested in a wind tunnel and altered accordingly. Even these days, the most sophisticated technology, computer software and virtual reality programs cannot create 'the feel' of car design like clay does.

The modellers responsible for my red Ford Escort Estate certainly didn't overtax their imaginations at the clay-car stage. It was not a beautiful object to look at, but at least it wasn't a Mini Metro. One thing is for sure, I could have done with a clay car when those lions were hurtling towards us at the safari park. Then I could have simply sculpted it back into place, so Alan and Robert would never have known anything about my little mishap.

At least the car was still going. I couldn't imagine having to go back to the laborious two-and-a-half-hour commute to and from Harefield. I did that for three whole years before deciding to resume driving lessons. Back then, I was young, enthusiastic and super-keen to impress my bosses. Which was no easy thing to do. If you remember, one of the two questions Robert put to me during my 'interview' was: 'What are you like at making tea?' I had answered 'Okay', yet the first time I made some, Robert took one look and poured it down the sink. He then made a cup himself and showed it to me.

'This is the way we make tea here,' he said. 'You might have made it differently in the past, but if you don't make it like this, you're in the canal.'

It sounds harsh, but that's how Robert and Alan were. And a few weeks later, they raised my salary from £45 per week to £75. My tea-making had passed muster and crucially, I hadn't been chucked in the canal. They must have thought I was fairly useful, I reasoned.

One afternoon, as I was going through my jobs, I had an idea how we might improve the way we went about things generally in the pottery. I thought I'd share it with Robert. He'd appreciate me showing some initiative.

Sadly, I can't remember what my sparkling idea was now, but Robert's response has stayed with me.

'Listen, you c**t,' he said. 'Whatever you think you've conjured up in your head with your one brain cell, I've thought of, contemplated, and binned before you had your first hard-on. So, shut the hell up and get on with what we tell you to do!'

As far as putting a person in their place goes, it was extremely effective. I was taken aback, I must admit, and imagine some people would have walked out if they'd been spoken to like this. But I didn't. Although I'm sensitive in many ways, I'm open-minded and swearing itself doesn't bother me. I understood that, in his inimitable way, Robert was just being honest with me, and I respected that.

I still forgot my place every now and then, thinking I had earned the right to progress. Later in the year, my bosses allowed me to start throwing simple shapes on the wheel and I thought they were finally giving me the green light to work on the production line with them – something I was itching to do, if only to sit down and have a bit of a rest now and then.

'When will I be able to get on the production line?' I asked Alan one day.

'Oh, I'd give it about five to six years,' he replied matter-of-factly.

*   *   *

Alan Pett and Robert Hudson were a couple of honest, no-nonsense blokes, definitely more Ford Escort than flashy Cadillacs. They could have been plumbers or electricians, but happened to be potters. There was no ego or pretence about them. They were true working craftsmen, who were very good at what they did. Alan was the more artistic of the two. After graduating in ceramics in 1966, he joined the Briglin Pottery in London's West End. Most studio potteries at that time were based in the countryside and made stoneware, but Briglin stood out, producing large quantities of domestic, white tin-glazed, dark earthenware with wax resist designs. It was all hand-thrown and decorated and because of this Alan had a great affinity with brush decoration. He became senior potter there, before leaving in 1977 to set up Harefield with Robert.

Between the two of them, there wasn't much more to know about studio pottery: different firing techniques, glazes, clay-body compositions, brush or surface decorative styles. I don't think I ever saw Robert relaxed. He was always thinking about how they could do things differently to improve the business. I didn't appreciate the word 'business' at all during those first couple of years, but it's certainly something I identify with now. Robert and Alan had created Harefield from scratch and maintaining it was bloody hard work. They certainly weren't going to let some tosser straight out of school tell them how to run the place.

What I learned from the two of them over the years could only have been achieved by starting right at the bottom, watching and learning from them. I was as green as the first leaf on a sapling tree, but what I did have was almost boundless energy and enthusiasm for learning the craft – and the nous to realise that these blokes could teach me a lot if I shut up and did what they said.

Ultimately, I wanted to be throwing pots and there I had a conundrum; as I was so busy with my other daily tasks, there was never any time to sit down and practise my throwing technique. So most evenings after I'd finished my work, I would stay behind and hone my skills at the wheel. I would routinely ball up 100 pieces and throw those into either a beaker or bowl shape. I would sit, concentrating like mad, determined to get it right. By the time I'd thrown fifty, I would be tired, but I had to keep going – fifty was nothing! It was simple repetition, the only way to achieve the consistency that is fundamental to a studio potter, ensuring you use the correct weight of clay to form the exact same shape, time and time again.

Once I'd finished, I would place all the pots on ware boards on a shelf for Alan to inspect. He would walk up to them with his ruler like an executioner with his axe. Anything that didn't measure up was binned (viewers of *The Great Pottery Throw Down* may recognise this practice). Alan passed sentence individually with a 'no', a 'yes' or sometimes, a 'what a c★★t'. It was exhausting, physically and emotionally, having thrown 100 pots and then seeing most of them summarily dismissed. It brought into focus exactly why I wasn't allowed to throw pots to sell; it could not happen until I had mastered consistency and speed.

Due to the amount of practice I put in, the 'yesses' gradually started to outnumber the 'no's. And then they virtually disappeared. I made it onto the production line and it had only taken four years, instead of six. I was elated and truly grateful to my bosses for taking a chance on me. Finally, I was a potter.

The only aspect of it I didn't like was the five-hour daily commute. I couldn't hack it anymore, so I forced myself to squeeze driving lessons into my busy schedule. The only 'window' I could find was on the way home from work, so I used to meet my driving instructor outside the Habitat store on Finchley Road and we would drive up to Golders Green. It was only a few miles, but seeing as it was rush hour on one of London's busiest roads, it would take an hour to cover that distance. I rarely got past second gear, but I did become an ace at close clutch control.

I remember the day my driving instructor told me I was ready to take my test. It filled me with dread. I felt sick. I was convinced I wouldn't pass. Despite the fact I was a singer in a band, I still had a fundamental lack of confidence in myself. I think this related back to my school days, the fear of exams and being told I was no good. Alan and Robert weren't a huge help, as they loved making a thing about my being Welsh, and whenever my test was mentioned, they would make some comment about Taffies not being able to drive and that I should stick to shovelling clay. The day before the test, the only advice they could give me was: 'Yeah, don't bloody crash,' followed by the inevitable c-word.

As it turned out, I breezed through the test and passed – first time. It sounds silly now, but I count that as one of the biggest achievements in my life. It was a mental barrier I had to break through and I came out the other side feeling stronger and more certain of myself than I ever had done. I could now drive to the job I loved in thirty minutes; life couldn't be better.

Oh, hold on. I didn't have a car.

It was a real downer having to make the journey in by foot, bus and train again the next morning. As I walked into the yard, I was surprised to see a car I didn't recognise. A red Ford Escort Estate. There was no one about, so I thought nothing of it and dutifully got on with my morning tasks. Around 9 a.m.,

Robert and Alan arrived and wasted no time in badgering me about my test.

'Fail then, did you, Taffy?'

'Nah. Passed …'

I felt proud of myself.

'Just as well,' said Robert. 'Because you see that car out there? It's yours.'

It took me a moment to comprehend what he was saying. The car was mine. They had bought it for me. It was their no-nonsense way of saying 'well done'. It was the first time I had ever experienced such a significant acknowledgment of my endeavours. Sure, I had won medals and cups for dancing, but this was much more meaningful; it was hard-earned. It was an affirmation – from a highly critical employer – that I was doing something right.

On that Monday morning, a couple of years later, when I drove the Escort into the yard all battered up by three lions, Robert and Alan made their remarks about Taffy drivers as I knew they would. But then they had a word with the blokes from the garage in the adjacent unit and within a couple of weeks it was as good as new. A few short years later, Windsor Safari Park went into receivership and closed. The lions went to the West Midlands to scare the shit out of people up there. The site in Windsor became Legoland. I've never bothered to visit.

7

'I'VE GOT SADE IN
TEARS NEXT DOOR'

Before I saw The Wigs, no man had ever touched my bollocks. It's not the sort of thing I wish to encourage. Keith, singer with this unruly band, finds them irresistible, however, and barely a gig of theirs can be endured without that claw-like grip making itself felt. Tonight he does it as a celebration, because this is a big night for them, and although they start with nerves by the bagful, they eventually shake themselves free, disporting themselves in a way only The Wigs can. Disgraceful, graceful.

– Mick Mercer, review of the Wigs at the Marquee Club,
Melody Maker, July 1989.

At this point, perhaps, I should warn readers of a nervous disposition that there is a bit of bollock biting in this chapter. Or rather, plenty of it. Pretend bollock biting, that is. Mostly. It was an act. In fact, it was *my* act. Maybe not an act I would adopt these days, but still … It helped get us some much-needed column inches in the music press.

Having read that review above, most if not all of you may be glad you never went to see the Wigs. We weren't for the faint-hearted, or those with sensitive hearing, or those with sensitive anything, to be frank. Mick Mercer's review conveys the havoc that ensued whenever we played, especially when there was a large, enthusiastic audience in front of us.

Here's more from Mercer:

With his hair fashioned into the shape of a mother hen [*yes, really*], Keith gives the soundman hell by first being utterly quiet and clenched. Suddenly, he spits water over guitarist Mick and a fracas ensues sending everyone into each other, breaking the spell. Keith lets rip and the sound goes haywire. He has a voice like a rocket bound for who knows where. Later he can be seen snapping his piranha teeth in Mick's groin, as he vibrates his lower portions. Poor bassist Stuart has his bum bitten. And all this from a band who have emotional highs even Bonnington wouldn't have attempted. The crowd certainly couldn't believe it, and by the end they were shrieking. Maybe it was fear?

The gig in question was our first ever at London's legendary Marquee Club. We did none of that shoe-gazing that was apparently cool at the time. We would grab the audience by the scruff of the neck and squeeze until we staggered off an hour later, sweaty and exhausted. We had come a long way since our first proper gig in 1984, and yet, perversely, you could argue we'd gone nowhere.

Let me back-pedal. Early in 1985, after a promising start, we had found ourselves down to three members when gorgeous, pouting bassist Nigel (who really did look like a rock star) had left to seek his fortune in the glam-punk scene. It was a real blow, as we'd been getting promising gigs at fashionable places like Dingwalls in Camden Market and the 100 Club in Oxford Street – places that also had decent PA systems, so I could actually, finally hear myself sing. The band had sounded good too, which made Nigel's loss extra hard.

Keith Cockburn, a junior doctor, replaced Nigel on bass and we also added Mark Rosario, a virtuoso lead guitarist whose faint resemblance to the singer out of Mungo Jerry led us to forever nickname him 'Mungo'. So now we had a load of extra noise, but we needed finesse. We booked the plush 313 Studios for some band rehearsals. They were expensive and at the end of each session we would pool our loose change and painstakingly count it into the hands of the exasperated studio manager. It was money well spent. Within weeks we were sounding better than ever and I was feeling more confident as a singer, too. That wasn't entirely due to the facilities at 313, however. Dear reader, I had begun taking singing lessons!

I had never really thought about lessons, and it was pure fate that led me to them. I was in a pub in Highgate one evening, having a pint or two, and got talking to some bloke about music. I mentioned I was the singer in a band. As you do.

'What are you called?

'The Wigs.'

'Never heard of you. Have you got a record?'

'No.'

Then he told me his mother was in the music business, and very successful. He said she was a famous singing coach.

'What's her name?' I asked.

'Tona de Brett,' he replied, a bit too smugly for me.

'Never heard of her,' I grunted, shaking my head and necking my pint.

That killed the conversation for a few minutes, but it got me thinking. I'd been suffering a lot of bad throats and I thought it might be related somehow to my singing. I put aside my pride and asked for my interlocutor's mother's number.

'She's not cheap, you know,' he warned, as he wrote it down on a taxi card.

'Good,' I said, getting the feeling that a lady named Tona de Brett would not appreciate a handful of loose change at the end of a lesson, and that I would probably never phone her.

A few days later, I was emptying my pockets and out fell the taxi card. On a whim, I decided to make the call. I had nothing to lose. A melodious, vaguely familiar voice answered and told me lessons were £25 an hour. I gulped. That was a third of my weekly wage. But I said yes.

When she answered the door of her lovely old Highgate house the following week, I suddenly realised exactly how I'd known her voice: she had been the coach tasked with teaching John Lydon (aka Johnny Rotten) to sing when he was in the Sex Pistols. She appeared in an hilarious scene in the film *The Great Rock 'n' Roll Swindle*, relating how Johnny could never pitch a note. She would later tell me that my pitch was rather good – well, better than John Lydon's anyway! However, I did little singing that first lesson. Instead, she introduced me to my diaphragm. Until that point, I hadn't even known I possessed one.

I didn't have too many lessons with Tona because, quite frankly, I couldn't afford them. But I did study long enough to learn how to project my voice without straining my throat, and that made a huge difference to our live act. Now, armed with a fully functioning diaphragm, I discovered a whole wealth of notes I could not only hold, but absolutely howl. I had to, after all, if I was to be heard over the rest of the band. God knows, we were loud.

On one occasion at 313 we were rehearsing in one of the smaller, pokey studios, because our favourite had been block-booked by another artist; a more important artist, maybe – certainly a more well-off artist. We were playing at our normal volume – as Spinal Tap would put it, 'one louder than 10'. There I was, midway through a howling roar of a note, when the studio door slid open and a narrow face appeared. A disapproving narrow face. We ground to a halt as this bloke, strangely swathed in a horrible nylon trenchcoat, trickled in. He looked like an insurance salesman, but introduced himself as Sade's manager. You remember Sade? Smoothie, jazzy, bland. Lovely Sade.

'Lads, lads, you couldn't turn it down a little, could you? I've got Sade in tears next door. Sade! Tears! She can't hear herself sing, and we've got a tour coming up.'

We almost felt sorry for him. I felt like offering to buy some insurance off him. But instead we stood there gawping at him, shuffling our feet and mumbling a few noncommittal 'okays' and 'poor Sade's'.

'I'd appreciate it, really, lads,' he said, oozing sincerity. 'And so would she.'

We nodded. Glenn the drummer issued a fierce drum roll. Mr Trenchcoat winced and then trickled back out of the door. The thing was, we didn't care about Sade's big world tour. We had paid good money to make our noise in the pokey studio, and make it we would.

'1, 2, 3, 4!'

The walls shuddered like never before. Mr Trenchcoat didn't come back. Sorry, Sade. Hope the tour went okay.

★　　★　　★

There were plenty of small London venues for bands to play back in those days, places where you only needed 40–50 people to create a great atmosphere. The indie scene was really sociable, too, and the people in other bands were our mates; we'd go and see them play, and they'd come and see us. There were no big egos. Well, it's pointless being a prima donna when you're making less than twenty quid a gig, isn't it?

We loved to play in the back room of the Pindar of Wakefield pub in Kings Cross. This unassuming venue had a real music pedigree: Bob Dylan had played at an open mic evening there back in 1962. Imagine that! The nights we played were promoted by Stan Brennan, a champion of the 1980s trash/garage scene, who had even produced a number of records, including the Pogues' first album *Red Roses For Me*.

One night Stan told us he was setting up a record label called Media Burn, and asked us to record a few tracks for a compilation album. A few weeks later, he had changed his mind and asked us to record a 5–6 track mini-album. We couldn't believe our ears – or our luck. We were going to make a record! The big time was beckoning!

There's something truly magical about the long-playing vinyl record. It's a design classic. I remember the thrill I used to get taking the Tube home with a brand new LP: reading the sleeve notes, gazing at it, first at the photographs of the band and then at the shiny, black disc itself. They are beautiful objects, full of promise and magic. Now I was going to make one myself and hold it in my hands.

We were booked to do the recording at Jacksons in Rickmansworth, where Motorhead recorded 'Ace of Spades'. That in itself was a thrill. Studio time there was exorbitant, which somehow made the whole process even more special. Entering Jacksons was like entering a church; we were in awe of it, and of the process we were about to undertake. I remember standing in the vocal booth with my 'cans' over my ears, feeling like a real rock star, and when we heard that first playback through the huge monitors in the control room, it was spine-tingling; this massive sound was *us*. And it sounded brilliant.

I have to say, the finished sound mix wasn't totally to our satisfaction, but our energy came across and the songs were good. We had high hopes when *The End of the Obvious* EP was released. However, Media Burn was a small label, even by indie record standards. Stan had zero budget to market the record and only 1,000 copies were ever pressed. So … from the start it was going nowhere – not that we knew that, at the time. We were green and keen. The record got a couple of good reviews from journalists whom Stan knew and then basically sank without trace. We shifted swiftly from the high of making and releasing a record to the low of the reality that not many people would ever hear it.

So we ploughed on. We got to hear about a new club that was making a name for itself, called Timebox, situated in the back of the Bull and Gate pub in Kentish Town. They were looking for bands, so Tesco-mince-counter guitarist Mick and I thought we'd head down one evening with a demo tape. We didn't know it at the time, but the person who ran the club was to become a true legend on the indie circuit.

His name was Jon Fat Beast, and he was an industrial unit to be sure; in old money, I'd say he measured about fifteen stone by five feet two inches. He wore vast coloured spectacles and cathedral-size T-shirts with band names printed on them. Most I had never heard of and some, like 'Bum Spanner', I suspect he'd made up to amuse himself and shock others. No matter what the weather, he wore a baggy pair of shorts, but then one rarely saw Jon outside the Bull and Gate to be honest.

We approached him in that humble, shuffling way that poor luckless bands hustling for gigs do.

'We're the Wigs,' one of us managed to utter. We waited for the excuses, the refusal, the 'sorry guys, I'm busy'.

'Oh, I know the Wigs. You're brilliant,' he said in a voice that wouldn't have sounded out of place on children's TV. 'Do you want a headline?'

We stood there grinning stupidly. But maybe the vicious bastard was toying with us?

'I can fit you in the beginning of April,' he offered.

'Er … yeah. April's pretty quiet for us at the moment,' said Mick, mentally consulting a fictitious band diary. And that was that.

At the Bull and Gate, we established our reputation for being a very good live band. It was an exciting time. The band had blossomed and on top of my lung-busting vocals, I'd come to develop an act. Yes, we're back to the bollock biting. And now I really will explain.

In early reviews, journalists made reference to the fact that I just stood still onstage. This needled me, but I didn't know what else to do. I could see that moving around a bit would liven up the crowd, and even the band, and make the whole spectacle more entertaining. But I was a potter. I spent hours each day with inanimate clay. I loved the quiet of objects. What could I do onstage that would work? I was big, not lumbering exactly, but … I needed to do something nobody would expect – not even me.

I can't remember at which gig it was, exactly, when I finally became animated onstage, but it was definitely during an encore of the old sixties classic 'Wild Thing'. It's a belter of a song, but with an odd instrumental section in the middle where generally I would stand around like a spare part. Then, one night, I sensed the time was right to liven things up. I jumped from the stage into the crowd and looked around for a likely accomplice. Spying a young lady with a twinkle in her eye, I let rip with some pelvic gyrations. She loved it. The crowd loved it. I went with it.

From then on, there was no stopping me and it became a feature of our set. I would jump into the audience, hips gyrating, to dry hump anyone who was willing. It was an act and part of the show, but also a little challenging, for me and everyone; I was pushing the boundaries to see what would happen. I was always half-expecting an angry boyfriend to smack me one.

Somehow, that never happened, but one night the dynamic changed in an unexpected way. When the moment came for me to leap offstage and find an 'accomplice' in the crowd, a bloke jostled himself into position. I couldn't avoid him. I decided to go with it, and thought of the most outrageous thing I could do, within reason. What came into my warped mind was to bite his bollocks … well, his general groin area. You know. So *that* also became my thing.

As Mick Mercer's review illustrates, I sometimes let band members have it, too. It sounds weird, unsavoury even, recalling it years later, but it was part and parcel of our performance and as time went on I developed that physicality further, rarely standing still for a moment. After a decent gig, I was usually covered in bruises. Once, I dived off a PA stack and landed on my knees. The next day I could hardly walk, but it was worth it, because the crowd had *loved* it.

Jon Fat Beast also loved us so much, he asked to manage us. We were thrilled when he started to plan a tour. We had never played outside London before and the prospect of going off on a bus around the country was so exciting. I wasn't sure how I was going to square it with Alan and Robert at Harefield, but I decided I'd worry about that when it happened. However, there was a problem, and it was something we had never considered in our haste to accept his offer of management; Jon was already run off his feet with the Timebox, putting on as many as eighty bands a month. He was over-committed.

The mooted tour started to shrink ... and shrink ... and shrink. In the end it amounted to two dates, one in Birmingham and one in Stoke-on-Trent – Burslem to be precise. Five people turned up to the latter and two of those left before the end. Upon our depressingly swift return to London, Jon admitted he didn't have the time to manage us anymore. It had lasted three months!

Jon kept the Bull and Gate going for a couple more years, but then found his real niche as MC for Carter the Unstoppable Sex Machine, often arriving onstage half-naked with obscene messages written on his huge belly. Bless him. He was a true legend and gave so many bands an opportunity to get up and do their thing. Tragically, he developed health problems in his forties and died of septicaemia, aged only fifty-two, in 2014.

RIP, you mad old bastard, Jon.

*   *   *

Jon was replaced as our manager by Chris Myhill. Chris was a breath of fresh air. In next to no time, his more diligent, understated approach promised to reap rewards. We made a single called 'Six O'Clock Shuffle' and, this time, the production on it was spot on. One review even used the word 'pop' in reference to it. To our utter astonishment, Radio 1 DJ Janice Long picked up on the record and on the evening of 26 January 1987, at approximately 9.40 p.m., the Wigs crackled over the airwaves for the first time. I sat by the radio waiting with my girlfriend and when the intro kicked in, I had this stupid great grin on my face. Afterwards, we all rang each other to make sure everyone had heard it. Of course we had! I've still got a tape of it somewhere.

Janice played it a few more times and then she invited us to record a live session for her – that was a real seal of approval. We went to the BBC's legendary Maida Vale studios to perform four of our best songs. Soon after the session was aired, 'Six O'Clock Shuffle' was Single of the Week in *Sounds* and we suddenly seemed to be everywhere. We thought our time had come. We were on the launch pad to stardom. But then, as before … nothing. Despite the radio airplay and great reviews, the single followed our previous efforts down the pan.

We were depressed. Dr Cockburn left, as he was now a proper doctor and no longer had time to be a failed rock star. He was replaced by Stuart Mitchell, Mungo's best mate. It was a stroke of luck; Stuart's confidence and enthusiasm rubbed off on us all and if anything, we improved in his first few months. Fundamentally, however, we remained stuck on the same circuit of gigs. Every now and then our manager's persistence would get a record label along to see us. I remember Polydor and EMI coming, but it was always the same result: 'Not commercial enough,' or, 'No image,' they would say. And they were right. Did I want this, or not? Why was I even in a band? What was it for?

By the time we got to play that gig at the Marquee in July 1989, it felt like we were swimming in circles. It didn't help that we were on the bottom of the bill. It was the first high profile gig we'd had in a while and we had to make it count. As we took the stage, Mick Mercer gasped at my hair: *the shape of a mother hen*. On the spur of the moment, I'd got some hair extensions put in. I had three springy antennas sticking out of my regulation flat top. It was decidedly 'different'. It was a laugh. It was fun and brought me out of myself and into a different persona.

We really went for it that night. I flung myself about like an overweight electric eel, assaulting my bandmates with my 'piranha teeth', stretching my larynx around longer and higher notes as the band played faster and more furiously. The crowd of around 600 was bigger than we'd usually play to and they loved it. It was nights like that which made it all worth it. Coming offstage with a sweaty, noisy crowd chanting your name is just the best feeling and impossible to describe if you've never experienced it. As we necked our beers backstage, we were buzzing. We'd gone down well and already the club promoter was talking about us headlining in the New Year.

1990. A new decade.

Maybe then the world would be ready for the Wigs? Or maybe then we'd recognise that music was only ever going to be about fun and friendship for our noisy, sweaty band.

8

EVEN THE RATS WOULDN'T MESS WITH THE FERRETS

So there I was one afternoon, totally immersed in making 200 of those delicate pots into which people like to plant their bonsai trees. I was chewing my lip and concentrating hard on centring a new ball of clay when I became aware, slowly, inexorably, of another presence in the room. I had worked at Harefield long enough to expect the unexpected and know that it wasn't always pleasant. I tensed, the hairs on my neck standing up, and raised my eyes from my wheel. It was then that I came face to face with something so grisly, the memory turns my stomach to this day.

Inches from my young, eager face there hung a dead horse's head, dangling in mid-air. Not just any dead horse's head, though; a skinned horse's head. Its decomposing tongue poked black and listless at me from a bony mouth that smiled in an awful, endless, lipless grin. The blind, dead eyeballs, meanwhile, stuck out on stalks, quite literally, reminding me of some cartoon character, electrocuted by an ACME gadget, mid-gag.

The clay flew off the wheel and I swore under my breath.

Slowly, carefully, I turned to look over my shoulder. There he was, grinning away like some hideous gargoyle come to life. Ron had come to visit. Ron was one of Harefield's special characters. I'm not sure people like Ron still exist.

'Hahahaha!' cackled Ron, as the horse's head continued to swing over my face. He was frankly delighted by his own rotten joke, didn't seem to mind that I had not jumped out of my skin. 'All right, are ya? Goin' to play yer banjo tonight, are ya? Yer banjo? Hahahaha!'

Life at Harefield was never dull, and mostly I loved it. I was now throwing alongside my bosses; not quite an equal, but making good progress. Between the three of us, we would knock out between 3,000 and 5,000 pots a week in an intense but extremely satisfying work regime. Every morning I would pug and ball up the clay, and we'd get through a ton of it on a busy day. In the afternoon, either Alan or Robert and I would sit on the wheels that faced out over the yard and throw. Robert would then do paperwork in the office or Alan would pack a kiln. None of us were ever idle for long. So these strangely frequent visits by some prize local characters were a welcome, if bizarre, intrusion into what was otherwise a very regimented day.

All sorts of oddballs, or should I say friends of Alan and Robert, would turn up to hang around and regale us with the ins and outs of their eccentric lives. Ron was a very good example. He was a short, stocky local man, with a thatch of black hair that looked as if it had been cut by a hay-baler. His teeth were rotten and his mouth was permanently smiling. He always wore a dirty mac and was usually carrying some part of an ex-horse. That wasn't simply eccentricity, though; he owned a large greyhound kennel. He and Robert, who owned dogs himself, would often go along to races together. Now, greyhounds love horsemeat, apparently, and Ron got it cheap and in bulk from a knacker's yard.

I once visited his kennels, and although I can't remember much about the dogs themselves, what I do recall is that he had this huge vat in the yard where he boiled down the various pieces of horse he'd been able to get his hands on. The process would create a sort of sludge for the dogs that came out of a large tap in the middle in great viscous, sinewy dollops. Apologies if you're eating.

I'd told Ron I was in a band and to him, for some reason, that meant playing the banjo. There was no other kind of music in his book. He was like a broken record when he enquired, every time I saw him, if I was playing my banjo that evening. I had to smile and nod, but often felt a bit like that poor horse that he'd dangled at me that day; grinning wordlessly, but with dead eyes.

Another regular work-day visitor I remember was John Lynch. He had worked at Barclays Bank with Robert, way back, and had been the branch manager before taking early retirement. Now, I have to say, a more unlikely looking bank manager you could never have met. You see, having retired, John was on a quest to become the most pierced person on Earth. Yes, piercings were definitely his thing. He had them in profusion across his entire face and they undulated when he talked and laughed. He also had them on his arms and chest, and apparently, quite a lot down below too.

We could hear him coming as he walked through the door; not from his footsteps, but from the muffled chinking of all his metalwork. He must have made a right old racket in the toilet. He finally achieved his piercing goal in 2009, at the age of seventy-nine, when he officially became the most pierced male in the world with close to 250 of them, mostly in his face and genital area. By this time his face was tattooed orange and black as well.

John's truly shocking appearance made him into a bit of a celebrity. He appeared in the TV sci-fi comedy *Red Dwarf*, as well as a lot of adverts. Underneath it all, unsettling as his appearance was, he was a genial, softly spoken man who was interesting to talk to, tea in hand. Oh yeah, and he wore sandals all year round.

I have always admired people who have the courage of their convictions and who want to step a little outside, or very far outside, what is considered 'normal' by society. As long as they're not harming anyone, I don't see why others should be outraged or shocked. Too many people waste their energy on being offended for the sake of it. To be different is good; it's merely another way of being creative.

*   *   *

I believed I had a job for life at Harefield, and I was fine with that. It may have come across to you by now that I love pottery. I have always loved the fact that when I walk into a room at a party or in a pub and somebody asks me what I do, I can answer:

I'm a potter. When I started out, it was an odd job compared to what most of my friends and acquaintances were doing, and I was proud of that.

I was a potter, and on top of that I was a singer in a band, which although not lucrative, was a really enjoyable and an important part of my life. It gave me balance; music was the yin to the pottery yang. And of course, there was the vague, slim glimmer of a chance that one day the band would take off, I'd become a mega-star and we could all retire to Rio. When all was said and done, I had a full and interesting life that I didn't think could be bettered.

Having said all that, I could have done without some of the stunts Alan and Robert pulled on me, especially in the early days. Besides the constant piss-taking and calling me a dumb Taffy, I would have to be on the lookout for their practical jokes, and they could be very creative, believe me. I remember once they left a ball of clay stuck to the wooden rafters directly above my bucket of water. As the ball dried out, it gradually shrank itself free of the rafter until it suddenly dropped like a bomb straight into my bucket, clattering like an explosion and sending water all over me. It also nearly made me quite literally poop my pants.

That was a good one. Less welcome was the time Robert came up behind me while I was throwing and shoved a pepper spray up my nose. I couldn't see for about half an hour. That's how I learned to throw blind … only joking. Or maybe I'm not.

Another memorable time, Robert made me a cup of herbal tea. I thought this was a bit odd, because he never usually made tea himself, and certainly not the herbal kind. Anyway, I thought I'd better be polite and, like an idiot, I smiled and said thank you and drank it. It was about twenty minutes later that I got an inkling something was amiss; my hands were actually growing. In fact, they were turning into enormous pink bananas. I had two great big bunches of bananas for hands. Yes, it had been mushroom tea, made from dried magic mushrooms, which Robert had made for me. I had never experienced it before (or since).

It was quite alarming, and continued to be so even after Alan explained to me what had happened and that I was simply hallucinating. I thought it best to continue throwing diligently, which believe you me was no mean feat – you try centring a piece of clay with a massive banana hand. Just try it.

Yes, that was a potentially dangerous situation and it was a stupid thing for Robert to do, but pranks like these, along with the unexpected guests, always kept things interesting. But everyone has their limit, and every now and then I had to put my size-12 foot down. I remember one day, when I must have been in a bad mood already, I decided I had to take drastic action. We were extruding tiles from the tile pug – we produced thousands of tiles in this way – when I snapped. I don't often get angry, but when I do, people know about it.

'If you take the piss one more time, I'm going to ruin every tile board we've just produced!' I shouted. I then proceeded to claw my fingers down the board we had just finished, effectively ruining the whole thing. That seemed to do the trick.

Despite all these distractions, welcome or otherwise, what we did best at Harefield was work. And boy did we work. To be a good production thrower, you need a thorough grounding in all the techniques required and to understand totally the different clays that you work with. It requires great tenacity, willpower and focus to be able to sit and make thousands of pots at a time. Through watching Robert and Alan and practising hard, I had acquired those skills; they helped turn me into a craftsman, and a proper potter.

We made and used our own clay recipe and we called it CH2. The recipe is secret, so don't ask. It was brilliant for throwing, incredibly plastic due to the particular ball clay that made up the majority of the recipe. As I've mentioned, I prepared all the clay. Preparation was key to the entire operation running smoothly and some orders required more of it than others. As well as the clay, I had to prep glazes and pigments, and sometimes even decal work (transferring pre-printed images or designs onto the ceramics). The more thoroughly I prepared, the smoother the production line would run. We got it down to a fine art, as we were always looking for ways to save time and money without compromising on quality.

For example, when I first started throwing in earnest at Harefield, we were making huge amounts of garden ware, or stoneware to be precise. This was mostly for garden centres. When it came to firing our bonsai pots – which were a really good seller – to save on space taken up in the kiln, we would 'set' these one inside the other. That way we could pack more in. As they were garden pots, we didn't have to glaze the inside of them, but like all clay bodies, there would be a certain amount of silica in the chemical make-up of the clay. Because of this, when we fired them, the pots would stick slightly on account of the silica melting slightly.

This could have been a problem, as we might have laboriously had to prise them apart. But Robert had a better idea. Instead, they were removed straight from the kiln into the back of the van, still in their sets. On the journey to the garden centre destination, what with all the bumps in the road, they would all knock about and shake themselves free, saving us precious time. And it's that kind of idea that earns you extra money.

As a rule, on a Friday, we'd fire up the big old oil-fired kiln. It was a right Frankenstein's monster piece of machinery, custom-built by Robert and Alan to their own specifications. They had integrated two old funeral burners to power the kiln and they were mightily effective. It was 250 cubic feet and could easily accommodate 1,500 mugs at a time. Because it got so hot, we tended not to throw on Fridays and besides, it could take up to five hours to pack everything into it. This was Robert's job. He knew the kiln like the back of his hand: where he needed to place certain ware in order to realise a particular glaze, finish or decorative effect. He made it into an art.

In fact he milked it a bit, to be honest, always taking an age to decide the best position for each piece while I stood around like a spare part. The kiln really made its presence felt in the studio. The two burners sprayed diesel oil into the kiln chamber at high pressure, which would set alight once making contact with the gas burners, shooting enormous flames down two trenches within the kiln. They sounded like rockets taking off once they were in full flow.

It was a trolley kiln, so the ware would all be packed onto a truck that ran back and forth on a railway track. Once it was ready, you'd push the whole stack forward into the chamber with the door attached to the truck. When you could push the truck no further, it was my job to clam up the door. This meant I would have to fetch the dreaded clam bucket that festered all the week in the studio. This was a foul-smelling concoction of slop and slurry that I suspect Robert and Alan used to piss in now and then. I'd have to grab handfuls of this rotten clay and press it into the cracks of the kiln chamber and door to seal it.

Like every task in the pottery, it had to be done methodically, leaving no gaps. The kiln had to be completely airtight to enable you to control the air intake during the firing. It took a day and a half to fire, so usually someone had to stay to adjust the burners at different intervals throughout the night. You'd sleep in a camp bed next to the kiln, so you'd never have to worry about getting cold.

One night, when we had a big job on, we all stayed there to load up and get things sorted. After firing up the kiln, we went to the local pub for a fairly large amount of refreshment. When we arrived back, I opened up the door and gave a start; one of the walls seemed to be moving. I knew I hadn't had enough to drink to be seeing things, so wondered briefly whether maybe I'd been slipped some more of the dreaded mushroom tea. I was reluctant to investigate.

When Alan turned the light on, all was revealed; the wall was crawling with hundreds of mice. They had discovered the cupboard where we kept sachets of baby food to feed our ferrets. The mice scattered the moment the light went on, but we let the ferrets out anyway. They were excellent at pest control and an absolute necessity with the studio being next to a canal, which was home to gargantuan water rats. We came into the pottery one morning to find they had killed our studio cat. In fact, it wasn't just dead; they had bitten its poor head off. But even the rats wouldn't mess with the ferrets.

Sometimes life as a potter can be a bit brutal!

★　　★　　★

I think it was around 1987 that Harefield started to produce tartan ware. I didn't know it at the time, but this range was soon to become Harefield's most successful, and in turn the catalyst for my departure. It's not that I didn't like it, though. Initially, we had made some large ceramic buttons in tartan for a new clothing range by Jasper Conran. They were cool. Tartan, in all its various permutations, is a real design classic. It never goes out of fashion, although at times it may be mega in vogue and then, at times, it may calm down a bit. It never completely disappears, and it always holds its head up. Robert and Alan realised this, and decided to apply the pattern to domestic ware in a range of bowls, plates, mugs, cups and saucers. It really took off.

It was exciting for me as a young potter to be involved in the creation of something new and then see it become a success. It was all down to Robert and Alan, though; they were very clever and innovative, and still are. They had devised a series of rollers to apply the tartan designs to the ware, with each tartan pattern requiring a different thickness of roller. I did a lot of the decorating using these and it required plenty of concentration and a steady hand. One false move and the biscuit ware would have to be washed off and you'd have to start again. Apply too much colour and it would spread and run everywhere; too little and there wouldn't be enough to cover the surface. All these mistakes were costly in terms of time and materials wasted, so I had to be on my toes, as ever.

Within a year we were producing huge amounts of this tartan ware. It proved very popular in the USA and we shipped a lot over there. The fact that it was handmade and hand-decorated was a big draw; people seemed to be attracted to the concept of the 'quality' that implied. I took note of this, half-mindful that one day, perhaps, I would come up with my own unique range.

Again, we found ways to speed up the process. I used a jigger and jolly for the first time to make some of the tartan ware. Put simply, this is a kind of throwing machine, which is useful when duplicating exactly the same shape over and over again. It was my first experience of semi-industrial pottery manufacture and made me appreciate the skill that is still required when using machinery. And it did help speed up the job when we were working to large orders. It was all going so well.

Then, out of the blue, on a dank and busy Tuesday afternoon, Robert mentioned, almost as an aside, moving the whole pottery up to Scotland. Had he really said that? Harefield, moving? To Scotland? I was horrified. I was speechless. I felt totally numb.

I could see the logic, of course; there was a big market for the products up in Scotland and property was far, far cheaper. It was a sound business move. But Scotland? I felt sick at the thought of it (not of Scotland itself, but of the move). It was so unexpected. In some ways, I saw my future – the future I had been half-planning, at least – being taken away from me.

Reflecting on this over the next few days, I told myself that Robert and Alan were too entrenched in their lives in Ruislip and Harefield to leave. They were Londoners through and through. Surely this would never come to fruition. For a few weeks I heard no more about it. But then it cropped up again. The Scottish Development Board were doubling whatever you could put into a business to encourage new start-ups. It was a really big incentive and I could see why this would appeal to Robert and Alan. They were both older than me and they had families. It was tough running the pottery at Harefield. They could see a better life for themselves.

One afternoon, not long after, I was making a handle for some tartan ware when Robert mentioned that he had found a place on the market just outside a town called Tain and that it would be perfect. It was an old RAF station. And yes, they were seriously thinking of buying it and relocating the whole pottery there. I had a look at the map; it took me a while, but eventually I found it. Tain was twenty miles north of Inverness! To me that was the middle of nowhere and then some.

They asked me if I would go too, which I took as a massive compliment. It was truly inspiring that they regarded me as an integral part of the team. But I couldn't go to Scotland. There was no way I was going to Scotland, no matter how much I loved working for them. My life was in London. My life was not only Harefield.

'Thanks for everything,' I said, shaking my head, half grinning and half crying, 'except the mushroom tea, you bastards. I'll never forgive you for that.'

Except I did.

After Harefield, I couldn't even consider looking for a job in another pottery. My seven years with Alan and Robert had been a unique and shaping experience in so many ways that I couldn't start again being bossed about by someone else. It was clear to me that I should start up my own pottery studio, even though I didn't have a clue how to go about it. It was my gut feeling; I had to start up somehow on my own. And it was scary.

It was a wrench watching them leave, that was for sure. I knew I'd miss the routine I had taken five years to establish, and I'd miss the job security. I'd even miss Alan, Robert, their mad friends and their vicious, sharp-toothed ferrets.

But it was time to move on.

9

A PIECE OF VICTORIAN LONDON STILL HIDDEN AWAY

I would not have achieved half as much as I have without the love and support of a number of people along the way. Looking back, I realise those who did step up to help were sometimes not the most obvious candidates. This was definitely the case when I started my own business at Highgate Pottery.

I was still going out with Jo at the time, and she lived in Highgate with her brother and parents. They hadn't held it against me that I nearly got their daughter eaten by lions at Windsor Safari Park. In fact, I got on brilliantly with Frank and Pat, Jo's parents. They were warm, down-to-earth, born-and-bred Londoners. There was no side to either of them and they were very accepting and welcoming of everybody; even me, and I was quite a handful back then. They were supportive of me learning the pottery trade, and even of me being in the band – up to a point. In some ways, they were more encouraging and easier to talk to than my own parents.

I remember how their lovely Victorian house was laid out over three floors, but they spent most of their time in an old-fashioned parlour just off the kitchen. Pat had a small but very profitable shop around the corner on Archway Road. I think she was probably the best shopkeeper I have ever come across; she was so efficient in everything she did and spot on with buying in products that would sell well.

Her shop was a cheerful little corner of the world, full of colour and scent: original last-minute gifts, zany T-shirts, incense burners, Indian jewellery, candles and all that hippy, Eastern, interesting stuff. This little treasure trove made enough money to keep the whole family and allowed husband Frank to pursue a fairly niche sideline of making reproduction spittoon buckets to sell at auction. Well, it takes all sorts, and I guess someone has to make them!

Frank had a workshop right at the top of the house and he'd spend all day up there polishing brass, varnishing wood and bringing together these lovely little curios, purely for the pleasure of it. He didn't make much money out of it – if you counted up all the time he spent working, the hourly rate would have been minuscule – but it was what he loved doing, and he was good at it. While I don't know where he learned his craft, he was

definitely a true craftsman, and I respected that. I think he possibly liked the fact that I was a craftsman, too. Frank was of the generation of people that were highly practical and could turn their hand to anything: electrics, plumbing, carpentry, spittoon-making. He was a man that was good with his hands.

When I told Pat and Frank about Harefield moving and that I wanted to set up my own workshop, they pointed me to a spare unit for rent in the courtyard behind the shop. The whole courtyard belonged to Richardson's, the fine old furniture shop that had been a fixture on Archway Road for years. I was intrigued and I took myself down there to give it the once over, not knowing what to expect, but not anticipating all that much.

The units were accessed down a very steep driveway that led into a half-cobbled yard that had once been extensive stables. It had a weird, forgotten feeling to it, like it was a piece of Victorian London still hidden away, almost subterranean. I could imagine the horses and hubbub that used to go on there, the shifty characters and stable boys. But now the stables had been converted into twelve workshops inhabited by a variety of craftsmen. It was strangely secluded and calm down there. Being below street level, it seemed to be insulated against the roar of the traffic only yards away on Archway Road. There was simply a quiet hum of people at work.

The unit that was up for grabs was less than appealing. In fact, it was in a terrible state. It had belonged to the carpenter who still had the next-door unit, but he'd used this one for storage. It was full of sawdust, damp and several years' worth of accumulated filth. The floor had bowed upwards and all the cobbles had been displaced due to the earth rising up underneath. But when I saw all this, it didn't put me off – it inspired me. My only thought was something like, 'fixing the floor, that will be my first task'. I had already made up my mind to take it. I wanted to make it work.

I was still at Harefield at the time, but I was determined not to hang around until they finally closed the doors and relocated to Scotland. I had to strike out on my own, and make the first, positive move. In a nutshell, it had to be me leaving before they did. And so it would come to pass: my final day at Harefield was the same as any other over the previous seven years. I did my work, Robert and Alan took the piss out of me as usual, and when it was time to go home, they said, 'See you later!' There was no standing on ceremony with those two, and I wouldn't have expected anything else. I drove away from there proud of the fact that in all that time, they had never managed to throw me in the canal.

I left Harefield with a specific and strong set of pottery skills, although I didn't yet have a business brain. I knew I would have to acquire one, however, and fast. For example, when Robert used to show me how to do things at Harefield, the process was always rushed, and I never knew why. He was often barely able to conceal his annoyance that he was being kept from something else, and that it was something more important. I didn't understand that when I was working for him, but once I started my own business, it all became clear: the buck had stopped with him.

I had been free to go home and forget about work at the end of the day (although I rarely did). But once it is *you* who's responsible for everything, there is pressure, and there is stress, and there is never enough time. There is always something else to do. For me, once I was working for myself, that would manifest itself in a voice chattering away in my ear that would keep me on edge: 'Nah, you're doing that wrong!', or 'You won't finish in time!', or 'Actually, what you've done is shite!' At times, it has become impossible to get rid of that voice. But I guess that's part of running your own business.

But here I was, just starting out. I was keen. In fact, I was desperate, and I had to get my new workshop into a fit working state quickly. Time for some business thinking. It all came together slowly over a period of several months, and I probably couldn't have done it without good old Frank's continued help. For starters, he and Pat lent me the money to buy my kiln. That was pretty key, I think you'll agree. And I had to have a good-quality, reliable kiln. I found one that would do the trick pretty easily – a Kilns and Furnaces model made in 1965, which was a very good year for kilns and potters!

However, there were two snags: firstly, it was only to be sold as one of a pair; and secondly, the school that was selling it was in North Yorkshire, over 200 miles away. But I wanted that kiln, God knows I wanted that kiln. I had to have it. So I did some thinking, my first with a business head on. It was painful but worth it. I reasoned that if I could sell the second kiln, it might compensate for the cost of travel and hiring a lorry big enough to transport them both back from Yorkshire. I gave it a go, and I was right. It paid off. I found a buyer for the unwanted kiln and was even able to drop it off on the way back down from the north. After what I was paid for it, my own kiln was effectively free. It was clearly a doddle, this business lark!

If only the removals part had gone as smoothly. I'd hired a lorry with a crane to load the kilns on and off, and it hadn't been a problem until I got back to Highgate and contemplated the steep slope down to the cobbled yard. I rubbed my chin. There was no way the lorry would get down there. What were we going to do? Again, I sought out Frank's input and together we devised a cunning plan. We would jack up the kiln on a pallet truck and tie a rope to the tow bar on my car. Then, at a snail's pace or even slower, I would back my car down the slope. If the rope broke or came loose, that kiln would hurtle down the slope and crash into the units opposite, taking out me or anyone and anything else in its path. That would not be good. Slowly, stealthily, we began the operation. I backed, the kiln moved, and amazingly, our plan worked. But that wasn't the end of our troubles.

When the kiln was safely at the door of my workshop, another problem suddenly occurred to me. It wasn't even a square peg in a round hole kind of problem this time; it was a huge great stonking kiln through the tiny eye of a needle kind of a problem. It would not fit through the door. For the next couple of days Frank and I toiled, taking the door and frame off and then carefully removing the glass wall from the front of the unit, brick by brick. It was a lesson in patience. It was also a lesson in insufficient planning. But then, finally, the kiln fitted through and joy was unbounded, for the short while until it was time to put everything back together again.

I said at the time that this was a major building job that I never, ever wanted to repeat – but in the end I did. I couldn't bear to part with the kiln and years later, when it was time to move on, I repeated the whole process. The kiln is still with me here by the sea and is in tip-top condition – which is more than can be said for me.

After that episode, Frank kindly offered to wire the entire workshop for me. He had been an electrician working in West End theatres and on racecourses, and he was decidedly old-school. Everything was done correctly and meticulously, and he wouldn't take a penny from me for it. He helped make the work benches as well. I did my share too, though; all the painting was me, and I'd decided that everything had to be white (my OCD kicking in there). In some places the paint failed to hide the great grey patches of damp, but I knew once the kiln was regularly fired up it would dry out well – and then remain dry.

It was around this time I was delighted to pick up an old Gosling and Gatensbury pugmill, made in 1953, for an absolute song. A good pugmill is essential for a production potter, as it allows you to recycle old clay. I've always added turnings and slops from my bucket to new pre-mixed clay. You throw it all together into the pugmill and it will turn out perfect clay salamis that are just the right consistency for throwing. I'll then cut that up according to what I'm making. For example, a two-inch slice of that is equivalent to a pound and a half of clay (about 680 grammes), which will produce a decent-sized cereal bowl. Not bad, eh?

It was all coming together rather nicely.

*   *   *

I thought my new landlord would be pleased with how I'd transformed the unit into a light, airy workspace. But no, Alan Richardson, a living, breathing Dickens character, was never one for pleasantries. I remember that he was slightly intrigued that anyone could make a decent living from making pots (I hated to tell him that I wasn't, yet), but all he was really interested in was my ability to pay the rent on time.

He was a right old character, was Alan. The Richardsons' furniture shop had been established by his father in the 1920s. They had become a very wealthy family and by the time I moved in, Alan was owner of a string of shops and properties along Archway Road. However rich he may have been, I have to say he was one of the meanest, most penny-pinching people I've ever met. And I don't mean that in a bad way – it was a fact. I found him extremely interesting from an anthropological viewpoint. I couldn't fathom how a man like him could exist in the late twentieth century. He belonged with the waifs and strays of *Oliver Twist* or *A Christmas Carol* with his permanent scowl and – despite his wealth – his extremely frugal lifestyle.

Where saving money was concerned, he had not a shred of pride. This man made it common knowledge that he got married on a Thursday afternoon because it was half-day closing and he wouldn't have to take time off. One day, I remember, he appeared at my door cackling away like a hyena. This was highly unusual and I couldn't imagine who or what could have caused this immense mirth. He could hardly breathe or speak for laughing as he shuffled in and pointed to his feet.

'These were free,' he managed to splutter finally.

I looked at him nonplussed. He repeated himself.

'I found these in a skip!' he said, indicating the worn and fairly ugly pair of beige shoes on his feet. 'They were free. Free!'

He was triumphant, as if he'd won the lottery. And then he wandered off again, still cackling. In all the years I knew him, I never saw him more happy than on that day.

When it was rent time, he would wander into the workshop rubbing his forefinger and thumb together in the almost universal gesture of 'Where's my money?' It wouldn't matter to him if I was in the middle of a conversation or the middle of a piece of work; in fact I could have been talking to the Queen and he'd rudely interrupt, with no hint of an apology.

'Where's my money?'

At least he was consistent, and in a way, I was very glad to be his tenant. Once it was all kitted out, I was really proud of my workshop. I decided to 'open up' for the first time one Saturday in April 1990. I'd had some A-boards made up and put them up on the main road to let people know I was there. Of course, nobody ventured down the deep dark slope that day to see what I was all about, but I wasn't too bothered; I already had plenty to do. Handily for me, Alan and Robert had passed on some local customers to me, which gave me a bit of a head start and brought in some income straight away.

My aim from the beginning was to produce purely functional ware: jugs, cups and bowls. I was never into free-form, artistic, conceptual stuff. I had my eye on this being a means to an end, a business I could earn a living by, so making things people used every day was logical to me. Because of my OCD, my designs revolved around the concept of uniformity. I loved making multiples of the same thing, like sets of beakers or bowls. I believed that was how I would make my living, especially as I knew I had the capacity to produce a lot of ware, and quickly. I was also naïve, I have to say, as I assumed there would be a steady stream of well-heeled Highgate types popping in regularly for a new dinner service or set of mugs. That, unfortunately, would never happen.

I loved being part of the set-up at Highgate. On a good day, central London was a ten-minute drive away and the North Circular road was only a mile up the hill, which was all very convenient for deliveries and those big West End orders I would no doubt soon be reeling in. Archway Road is the old Northern Road, the A1000, and is still the main route for goods lorries coming down from Scotland into London, which was good news for me as things transpired.

You see, as things turned out, Robert and Alan's new pottery in Tain was very close to a salmon farm that used to send produce down to Billingsgate fish market every week. We made a little deal that would allow me to get my hands on some of their excellent clay on a regular basis. So every month or so, Robert would call the fish farm and get their lorry to bring a ton of the CH2 clay down to me. The lorry would drop off the fish at Billingsgate on the Isle of Dogs at 3 a.m., then stop off at Archway Road on their way back up north. The driver would call me around 4.30 a.m. and I'd wait by the side of the road with a sack barrow.

The stench of fish would knock me sideways when he opened the back of his juggernaut, but it was a small price to pay. I was, after all, getting a free clay delivery from 600 miles away. Ferrying a ton of clay up and down that slope with a small barrow took some time, I can tell you, but there was no traffic around at that time of the morning and it was a great way of keeping fit.

*   *   *

Although I was still, theoretically, living at home with my parents, I was spending most of my time either at the workshop or at Jo's house, which was two minutes round the corner, or at Pat's shop, which was next door and handy for a cuppa. So it's fair to say that the only time I left Highgate around then was to rehearse with the band at 313 Studio in Holloway, or to go out to play a gig. And pretty soon, that stopped too. Let me explain.

It's not that there was any huge row about musical differences, or girlfriends, or royalties, or drugs or poor backstage refreshment. We were still mates and having fun, but in some ways, the spark had gone. I think it finally dawned on us that we were never going to make that magic leap into the big time, and the alternative was not worth us continuing. Things came to a head when we played a gig at the Camden Palace to over 1,000 people, which should have been fabulous, and we were shit. We had nothing more to give. That was it; we called it a day and moved on.

We'd had some great moments together, mainly onstage, but the Wigs had never been able to break out of those small club gigs, or bag ourselves a proper record deal. We didn't help ourselves by rarely venturing beyond London to play, although without records to promote that was a risky step to take. Taking a critical view, all these years later, I'd suggest we didn't want it enough; none of us were prepared to go that extra yard to give it a real shot. We all kept on proper jobs throughout the years we were together, and I certainly never considered giving up mine. Setting up the pottery had shifted my priorities irrevocably; I could see the way ahead and there would be no time for further rock 'n' roll shenanigans.

We decided to give it one more go for a farewell gig, so we could say goodbye to our diehard fans (and yes, we did have some). We duly booked ourselves in at the good old Bull and Gate and promoted it. However, when the big day came, the gig had to be cancelled at the last minute as an administrative error had left the club temporarily without a music licence. It felt quite fitting, our farewell gig being cancelled like that.

We wouldn't be quashed, though. We rescheduled it and, shortly before Christmas 1990, we played our last gig. It was an emotional night. I remember fans trying to persuade us, after the show, not to split up. But the time was right.

The Wigs had left the building.

★   ★   ★

All my attention now turned to the business of making and selling pottery. I had quickly settled into life in the yard, which was a hive of activity, although in an understated, calm kind of way.

Those who worked out of the other units had mostly done so for years and they went about their business seemingly unconcerned by the outside world. It was a genuine creative hub, as they would call it these days.

Tony ran his carpentry workshop next door to me. He had several people working for him, so there was a constant stream of chatter and laughter filtering through the wall, which I found comforting. He ran his business by the seat of his pants – we were all like that to a greater or lesser degree, but Tony was definitely in the 'greater' category. There were often men in suits from the VAT office or similar buzzing around the buildings looking for him. It was entertaining to watch him convincing them they'd got the wrong place, or even that 'Tony' wasn't around.

Another carpenter, Dave, had been a tenant since the early 1970s. He kept a fire going constantly in the yard all year round, fuelled by offcuts from the latest job he was working on. When I think of the yard now, I recall the wonderful aroma of wood smoke. Ray, the furniture restorer who worked in a small workshop across the yard, was always busy bringing old family heirlooms back to life. Harry ran the painting school up at the top of the yard. He had the best workshop, in my opinion, as it was split level and spacious with a high ceiling. These guys weren't shouting from the rooftops about being 'artisans'; they were simply craftsmen quietly going about their work.

These units were increasingly rare in London, so no one gave them up and the make-up of the yard remained constant over the years. We watched each other go through good times and bad times; people got married, had kids, loved and lost. We were a little community, tucked away unseen in the middle of London. As time wore on, every summer I would host a barbeque, fixing up fairy lights across the yard, and we'd cook and eat under the canopy of the rowan tree that presided over us. Some of the residents used to come down from the flats above Richardson's and join us. The place had a great atmosphere, and I had some of the nicest times I can remember while working and chatting there.

I had no idea when I started that it would take me so long to make the business work, financially. Perhaps it was better that way, or else I might not have persevered. Early on, the man who made my pottery stamps offered me the following pearl of wisdom, spitting it out in his broad cockney accent: 'As long as yer plus side's bigger thun the minus side when you come to tally up, yer doin okay.'

I smiled and nodded politely at the time, but I would find out the hard way that this was easier said than done.

As for Frank and Pat, well … within a couple of years Jo and I split up and, as you do when you're youngish and freeish, I moved on and tried to forget about it. I don't remember talking to Pat and Frank again after that, which was a great shame, but one of those things. Looking back, I realise I had a better relationship with them than I did with Jo in some ways. The last I heard, they had sold up and moved out to Hertfordshire to seek a better, quieter life for themselves, which I hope they found.

Without them, I wouldn't have ended up in that yard alongside those other craftsmen, where I would spend fifteen happy, productive years. And if I didn't make it clear at the time, I hope they know now, wherever they are, that I am truly grateful for their help.

10

STARING INTO THE ABYSS

One filthy evening in 1993, I fell into my Highgate workshop and slammed the door behind me. You could say I was pissed off. I had just crawled through five miles of rush-hour traffic at the end of a tedious day spent delivering parcels. And it wasn't as if business was booming. Far from it. I was working as a courier part-time to supplement my meagre income. I was knackered, but had an order that needed preparing for the morning. It was going to be another brain-numbingly late night. At least the kiln had kept the workshop toasty, but it didn't lift my mood.

As I glugged my tea and poured another cup, I gazed right through the massive stack of bowls in front of me, waiting to be boxed up. I was looking into my future and it didn't look great. In fact, it looked like a load of bone-crushing work for virtually nil return. I put down my tea and made a decision. To hell with the bowls, I thought, I am going to work out, right here and right now, exactly what I should do to lift myself out of this rut. It was indeed going to be another late night.

I raked back over my journey so far as a potter, searching for answers and inspiration. Why was I doing what I was doing? How could I make it work?

When I started at Harefield Pottery, I lacked nothing in confidence. In fact, I was a right cocky bastard. As far as I was concerned, all I needed was some experience to enable me to apply my brain-full of A-level knowledge, and I'd be made. Within weeks, Alan and Robert had mercilessly picked that half-baked theory apart, and my re-education was underway. Besides all the practical stuff relating to the objects we were producing at the pottery, they were keen to teach me that it wasn't all about pots and mugs and — if you liked that sort of thing — decorative ceramics. I was ignorant about the various industrial uses of this versatile raw material I was now dealing in. I knew the space shuttle was covered in 30,000 ceramic tiles, which allowed it to re-enter the earth's atmosphere safely, but it didn't seem relevant to me.

One afternoon, Alan showed me a picture of this bloke in a flat cap, 30 feet in the air, suspended on a crane. It looked as if he was poking a hockey stick into a 20-foot-long piece of clay that was dangling from the ceiling by chains. On closer inspection, I could see he was hand-turning threads into this clay. It looked like he was making a gigantic clay screw. Alan explained that the man worked for a pottery company called Allied Insulators and was making porcelain electrical insulators for a power station. This was no decorative ceramic.

Like me back then, you probably don't know what a porcelain electrical insulator is exactly. Why should you? Think of one of those electric substations you must have passed on the motorway, where they have rows and rows of what look like giant springs projecting upwards from the transformers. Those are electrical insulators. Porcelain, I learned, was a highly effective insulator of high-voltage electric current, one of the constants in the supply networks since the early days of electrification. In this roundabout way, Alan was giving me a lesson in what clay was capable of; and I was getting to understand better its strengths, limitations, and almost infinite possibilities.

Initially, insulators were made of glass, but they proved inadequate when the rapid expansion of electric power distribution in the 1880s required higher voltage power lines. Porcelain was known to be a superior – if more expensive – insulator, so the development of a more efficient alternative was taken up by the master potters. Merely switching to porcelain wasn't enough; a high-performance material allied to radical design was needed to withstand up to 10,000 volts. It was William Cermak, a Czech-born American, who cracked the design in 1893, when he developed the distinctive 'petticoated' porcelain insulator, recognisable as the one with me in the photograph, and still widely used today.

Cermak's breakthrough, however, wasn't enough to earn him the coveted title of 'Father of Porcelain Insulators'. Oh no, I hear you cry. That accolade goes to New Yorker Fred M. Locke, whose experiments with various clay mixtures at the Imperial Porcelain Works of Trenton, New Jersey led to his development of 'wet process porcelain', a mixture that proved most effective in standing up to high voltage service in all kinds of weather conditions. Using this method, the porcelain is mixed wet, plunged in a mould and then shaped on a wheel or turning machine. It is dried, glazed, and fired at very high temperatures. This porcelain lacks the small holes and cracks typical in the drying process previously used.

These breakthroughs, combined with a colossal demand for electricity, spelt huge profits for companies producing porcelain insulators at the turn of the twentieth century. Companies like Allied Insulators, or Buller's Limited, as they were then known.

Their story began in 1842, when Captain J. Buller and Mr J. Devett bought the Folly Pottery and started the Bovey Tracy Pottery Company. Within twenty years, they had moved the business to the heart of the pottery industry, establishing themselves in Hanley, near Stoke-on-Trent. They were one of the first companies in the world to see the huge potential in electricity, and by the end of the century they were supplying porcelain insulators in huge quantities across the globe. By 1920, they had outgrown Hanley and to meet the ever-growing demand for their products, they built a larger, better-equipped factory at nearby Milton.

You might be wondering what all this has to do with the price of clay, but stay with me, I will return to Highgate Pottery, and there will be a point to this seemingly random time travel. Enjoy the ride; it will make sense, trust me.

Soon after Buller's move to their new state of the art facility, students from the nearby Burslem School of Art began to show an interest. The principal, Gordon Forsyth, was a notable ceramic designer and pivotal figure in the local pottery industry. He used his considerable influence to persuade Buller's to supply the school with hard paste porcelain. Also known as 'true porcelain', this is the most common type of Chinese porcelain and it was incredibly difficult to come by in Britain at that time. Buller's used it to make their electric insulators, so they had more than enough to spare the lucky students.

In 1934, Forsyth went a step further and proposed Buller's open their own ceramics studio, which they duly did. It was a coup for Forsyth and the school, allowing them access to the company's technicians and cutting-edge kilns. The combination of Forsyth's reputation, the expertise of Buller's staff and unlimited supplies of high-quality porcelain created a 'perfect ceramic storm', which attracted the country's most talented potters. Over the next eighteen years the studio would thrive, gaining a reputation for innovation and the manufacture of outstanding industrial pottery and decorative wares.

There were two people key to the success of the studio. The first was Guy Harris, a Buller's director and company chemist; there was nothing he didn't know about glazes. The other was Agnete Hoy, and the story of how she ended up in Milton in the first place is pure kismet. She was born in London to Danish parents during the First World War and the family returned to Denmark when she was seven. Her parents were artistic and encouraged Agnete to pursue her interest in ceramics. She studied at Copenhagen College of Art and Crafts and it was here, in 1939, working under Danish potter Natalie Krebs, that she gained invaluable experience working with high-temperature porcelain.

Later that summer, she was visiting her brothers in England when war broke out and she was effectively stranded for the duration. Needing to find work to support herself until she could return home, Agnete teamed up with her brother Svend, who was working as a potter in Stoke-on-Trent. Never short of confidence, she aimed high and took her portfolio along to Wedgwood. They had no opening for her, but referred her instead to Gordon Forsyth who, in turn, introduced her to Buller's. Her work and ideas impressed them, as did her knowledge of their porcelain, and Agnete Hoy was appointed head of their studio, aged only twenty-six.

With the support and know-how of Guy Harris, Agnete nurtured what had been a small design studio and created something unique: a bold, innovative company that bridged the gap between industrial ceramics and studio pottery. It helped, of course, that Buller's could afford to give the studio free rein. Without financial or creative restraints, Agnete was at liberty to experiment, and in tandem with her bold designs for mass production, she would go on to produce some exquisite one-off ceramic pieces. She was always open to new ideas and would frequently invite influential studio potters such as Bernard Leach, his son Michael, and Rosemary Wren to visit. In these benign circumstances, the studio fizzed with artistic and intellectual intensity, and was unlike any other at the time.

Buller's must have been a wonderful studio for a young, enthusiastic potter to work in, like Harefield had been for me. But now I was on my own, a capable potter, but a rookie businessman, scarcely able to cover my basic running costs; and the fact I was able to manage even that, I owed more to Alan and Robert than I cared to admit. Before moving their pottery up to the Scottish Highlands, they passed on a few of their clients to me, mainly the ones they could no longer be bothered with.

One of these was Pulbrook and Gould, a high-class florists in Sloane Street, Chelsea. Run by Lady Sarah Pulbrook, they had provided 'an exclusive and elite service to a discerning international clientele', since 1956. This included the flower arrangements for a number of royal weddings. It wasn't a bad account to hold. Lady Pulbrook (who died in 2011, aged 105) was an exacting but loyal customer. My problem lay in finding more like her. I was like a hopeless juggler with too many balls; unable to generate any balance or momentum. Crucially, I lacked the time and skills to market myself, and without this I plodded along, staring into the abyss that was my bank balance.

That was why I had taken up the kind offer of my mate Anthony to go and deliver parcels for his company Abis Brand Couriers (he had done well for himself since the old Tesco days). It was only a temporary arrangement, I told myself, until I could find my feet. But here I was four years later, sitting in my workshop in the early hours, trying to fathom a way out of it. I wasn't about to start making millions from porcelain insulators. Could I be another Agnete Hoy? What could Keith Brymer Jones actually be about?

The answer was right in front me; literally. I had picked up a ceramics magazine and was vacantly thumbing through it when my eyes fell upon an advert in the back pages: 'Creative Clay workshop – £150'. That was the sort of money I was making delivering parcels. But it would be way more fun. And it was something I was passionate about, too. Could I, perhaps, run a workshop? I pondered this question as I finally got around to packing up the pots.

First thing the next morning, I got busy putting out adverts and contacting numerous schools and day centres and, lo and behold, within days, I got a call back from a special-needs centre in Edmonton. They were keen for me to run a weekly workshop for their clients, and I jumped at the opportunity.

The only snag was, I had never had any meaningful contact with people from this client group. My first session was a bit of a rough ride; I was unprepared for the pandemonium that broke out when I was introduced to them. The introduction of the clay then ramped the level up a notch. Had I made a mistake? It was about as far as you could get from the order and sophistication of Buller's studio.

I decided to keep things simple, asking the class to make their favourite animals or favourite food, but this was taken literally by some students. who thought lunch had come early and started to tuck in. Others chucked it about the room or made clay tits and cocks, but they clearly enjoyed the session. The day centre staff were amazing. I wondered at their patience, their tolerance and understanding of the behaviour and needs of their clients, many of whom could be very challenging. Nothing fazed them.

Following their example, I soon became more relaxed around the students, although there were still times when I had to learn the hard way. Take Jeremy, for instance. He loved my classes. He'd get so excited when he saw the clay that if I was nearby, he would grab my hand. I came to understand this was his way of expressing his joy and enthusiasm. One day, I can't remember what we were making, but he was *really* enjoying the class and I was *really* enjoying him enjoying it. That is, until he suddenly bit down hard on my thumb.

It was agony. He might have bitten my thumb off if staff hadn't dived in. It taught me always to keep on my toes, look out for the signs, and anticipate the triggers that preceded these extremes. After all, I couldn't afford to lose a thumb, no matter how much fun we were having.

I loved running those sessions and of course, it meant I could finally give up the courier driving. Buoyed by the realisation that I could pass on my knowledge and enthusiasm to others while earning money too, I began running evening classes from my studio. I loved the social aspect of having people from different social backgrounds coming to visit me once a week. I had nurses, a judge, a sandwich-bar owner and a publisher, all of them brought together by a collective need to create and use their imaginations. It was heartening to see people throw off the worries of their day at work and get lost in clay. It reminded me why I fell in love with it all in the first place.

I finally had financial breathing space and time to think about my next move. In the early 1990s, homeware had started to become fashionable and the big department stores had begun stocking larger, more diverse ranges that changed with the season. I saw this as a real opportunity to cut in on their supply chain. Because of my training at Harefield, I was capable of throwing large numbers of pots on my own, quickly, and reasoned that if I could only get a foot in the door, I could cope with supplying these larger retail outlets.

I needed to come up with a simple, repeatable design. Picking up one of my pottery books for inspiration, I stopped at a page with some sgraffito bowls made by Lucie Rie, someone I would often turn to when I needed inspiration. She is a towering figure in British ceramics, even though, like Agnete Hoy, she arrived from abroad shortly before the Second World War; in her case, to escape Nazi Austria.

The sgrafitto technique is a fairly simple one, produced by applying different layers of colour (underglazes or coloured slips) to leather-hard clay and then scratching off the top layer to create contrasting images, patterns and textures that reveal the clay colour on the bottom layer. I set about designing my own bowls using this technique, keeping the pattern as simple as possible so I could replicate it easily. I was really chuffed with my results, more so than with any of my previous designs. I had achieved what I had set out to do, and truly believed these bowls would not look out of place in the major retailers. I was convinced, but would they be?

I took what I thought were very tasteful pictures of my new bowls and then sat down to think where I should send them. I decided to try Heals, an upmarket homeware store on the Tottenham Court Road. One of the reasons for this was because the 134 bus went past Heals and also stopped outside my workshop, so when I dropped my envelope at their front desk, I was back at work within the hour. I didn't hold out much hope of hearing from them.

Two days later, my phone rang.

'Is that Keith?'

'Yes. Keith Brymer Jones.'

'Gill Grundy here. I'm the ceramics buyer at Heals. I'm looking at the photographs you sent in of your work. I love the bowls.'

'Oh. Great.'

Gill cut to the chase.

'How many do you think do you think you could make?'

'Well, how many do you want?

I braced myself for the unreasonable request I felt she was about to make.

'Do you think you could possibly make three hundred, say, in three months?'

Elation! I could throw that many in one morning and turn around the whole order in ten days.

'Yes, I think I could manage that.'

She was delighted.

'This is fantastic!' she gushed. 'Three hundred handmade pots in three months.'

And that was how I got my first real lucrative customer. The first order sold out rapidly and they placed another, bigger one. I added to the range and Heals stocked it for the next four years. Getting that first big customer really boosted my confidence; at last, I had a decent regular income and I had gained some valuable insight into how the buyers' system worked. Word spread that I was reliable and able to turn around large orders of quality handmade ceramics in good time. Over the next year, I would be asked to supply other major high street retailers such as Habitat, Monsoon and Laura Ashley.

Here's where Buller's comes back in; I discovered that Heals had also been a customer of Buller's in the early 1940s. Agnete Hoy had visited herself to try to sell them some of her pots. Heals did not take them, but instead asked her if she could produce a range of porcelain animal models for sale in America, where there was a big demand for them. I have looked these up online and they are collectors' items, a world away from the parent company's ceramic electric insulators. Despite its excellent reputation, the Buller's studio never made any money and it was closed down in 1952, quite suddenly, with all its remaining stock sold off cheaply.

In 1959, Buller's and another British insulator manufacturer, Taylor Tunnicliff, merged to form Allied Insulators. They remain an innovative and respected company, worldwide. Agnete Hoy went on to work at the Doulton Lambeth Studio, and when that closed in 1957, she set up a workshop in her home in Acton, just round the corner from where Abis Brand Couriers was based. It's a small world!

11

'MAY I BOTHER YOU FOR SOME MILK?'

My workshop, despite being so close to the relentless thunder of traffic on the Archway Road, could be surprisingly tranquil. In the evenings, with twilight at the windows after everyone in the yard had gone home, the only sound would be the occasional click of the contactors on the kilns kicking in and out, regulating the temperature. The sound was comforting, like the ticking of an old clock. Alongside it, I could hear myself think.

It was like this when Jane, my bereavement counsellor, would come to see me, as summer faded into autumn in late 1994. Once a week, just before 7 p.m., I would sweep the studio floor and put out two chairs in the middle of the room, facing each other. At first, I viewed our meetings as an inconvenience and an unnecessary distraction. I was, after all, a workaholic, driven by a compulsion to make myself a master potter and a successful business. It felt awkward, speaking to a stranger about personal things; or speaking to anyone about personal things, for that matter. But seeing as Jane was a counsellor, it seemed pointless us both sitting there in silence, breathing in the clay dust as the sparrows chattered outside.

One of Jane's first questions was very simple: what got me up in the morning?

'Anxiety,' I replied, without hesitation.

As we talked, in my case pretty falteringly, it became clear I had been living in a state of anxiety for some years. Constant worry and fretting over not making enough money to pay the bills, let alone myself, was a default setting I had learned to live with. Only now, I was no longer able to live with it.

A few months earlier, in the spring, I would have laughed off any suggestion I would be receiving counselling before the year was out. Brit Pop was having it large, Blur and Oasis were just limbering up, my life was good and the business was taking off. Added to this, I had a set idea about counselling and those who needed it. I associated it with being weak. I was convinced that if you had a problem, the way to get over it was to get your head down and work harder. You had to push on. And not discuss it. After all, that was what I saw my parents do. Besides, what could go wrong?

That spring I was a nomad with regards to my domestic situation. Occasionally I would stay the night in my old room back with the folks at Walmington Fold, which still had the Bauhaus and Lucie Rie posters on the wall. It had been a happy place when I was growing up, but it felt strange going back there now and that feeling of family comfort had dissipated. My parents, by then, had largely given up trying to communicate with each other in any meaningful way, and seemed content to play out their time in silence.

Here's an illustration of what it was like, from my point of view. One night I came back there after a Bauhaus gig at the Lyceum. It had been a great night, I was feeling pumped up and inspired. As I opened the front door, I was greeted by the now-familiar sight of my mother labouring up the stairs after another night on the sherry. Sherry was her counsellor. I was still making my helloes when, halfway up, she lost her balance. As I looked on from the front hall, she tumbled in slow motion back down the stairs. What are the chances? I can still hear the dull crack as her head hit the radiator at the bottom.

Rushing to her side I feared the worst, but miraculously, she was fine: in fact, she was so pissed she hadn't felt a thing. She resisted my suggestion of phoning an ambulance, so I helped her up and put her safely to bed. Then I charged back downstairs to confront my father, who was still seated in front of the TV, happily watching the football. What followed was one of the few times in my life that I really let rip. I told him his attitude towards my mother was disgusting, and that he had a complete lack of empathy or concern for her. I didn't spare him. But this scene did little to change anything. They were both firmly stuck, each in their own 'marriage stress crack', which were too wide and too deep for any escape.

Given this situation, most nights I would find somewhere more cheerful to lay my head, often on the sofa of my mate

Anthony at his flat in Notting Hill. Living part-time out of a bag and not having a place of my own did not bother me; I was resilient, made of rubber, not pottery, and the workshop was my world. All the possessions I needed, which defined me, if you like, were there: my kilns, my pottery wheels, the trusty Gosling and Gatensbury pugmill and, believe it or not, the biggest raku plate − or platter, or tray, or salver − you will ever have seen.

★   ★   ★

I knew I had to have it, the moment I set eyes on it. It was on a day trip to Brighton, sometime in the mid-eighties, and I was on a bit of an adventure. It was love at first sight. There it was, lying on the floor of John Dunn's studio, under the arches on the seafront. The plate was not on display or anything, but there was no way you could miss this whopper − it was over half a metre across. Just think about that! I picked it up to have a closer look. The finish bore the hallmarks of the unique reduction firing process used in its creation: a beautiful, lustrous metallic sheen on the front, contrasting starkly with a reverse that had been blackened by smoke and flame.

For me, this plate was a perfect example of raku. It was spectacular; a one-off that could never be replicated. And John let me have it for forty quid. It was a bit of a stretch for me, back then, but it was money well spent. That plate has taken pride of place at my workshop ever since.

Now, raku is arguably the most unpredictable process you can attempt in pottery, though undeniably it is also one of the most accessible and fun. The whole process is speeded up compared to a normal firing: the kiln is heated quickly, the pottery is removed from the kiln while still red hot and then cooled down rapidly. You fire at a low temperature of 900 degrees centigrade, which is not hot enough to vitrify the clay. As a result, raku ware is more porous, less dense, and lighter than pottery fired at a regular temperature. This also means it is more fragile and unsuitable for use as functional ware. John Dunn's plate is not for eating off, but it looks fantastic and it has great character, and that is what raku is all about: visually stunning decorative ceramics.

The finish on John's plate was achieved through a reduction firing. To do this, you whizz the red hot pottery out of the kiln and into an airtight container, nestling it in among some combustible material such as paper, sawdust, straw or feathers. As these materials burn, they consume the oxygen in the sealed space and this creates carbon monoxide. This in turn draws oxygen out of the clay and glaze, making them denser and causing the textures and colours to react and intensify.

A raku firing can be completed in an hour or two, and as you are firing at low temperature, it is even possible to build your own raku kiln. All you need is a metal dustbin, some ceramic kiln fibre to line it, a propane gas tank, a propane torch and a pair of tongs. You cut an air vent in the top of the dustbin, another in the side (for the torch) and you're all ready to go.

Of course, due to the unpredictable nature of the firing, there is a high casualty rate for raku, and for every spectacularly successful piece you complete, you may have quite a few that collapse into a jumble of pretty, broken pieces. Whenever you expose pottery to rapid changes of temperature there is the risk of 'thermal shock' – which can be catastrophic. You can only hope this will not manifest itself as an explosion, but rather the surface crazing and crackling in the effect that is unique to raku. As any middle-aged man will tell you, crazing and wrinkles add character and charm. It has taken me many years of life, stress, worries and shock to acquire the lines on my face, but John Dunn's plate was born – perfect – with them already in place.

*   *   *

In 1994, I was twenty-nine and still baby-faced. I was no stranger to stress and anxiety, but until that summer it had been fairly superficial, relating to the pressures of work, or maintaining relationships, or not having much money. I had experienced no real personal trauma. But one simmering June afternoon, Thursday 30th to be precise, that was all to change.

It had been a hectic day. I had been making the most of the long summer days: getting in before 7 a.m., emptying and filling the kilns, then throwing like a maniac to keep on top of the orders coming in. With that all finished, I had to prepare the workshop for that evening's pottery class. I was now running these three times a week, with five students coming along to each. It does not sound like much, but it was keeping me afloat financially. It was an enjoyable way to earn extra income.

My students all understood and respected each other regardless of their ability, and this created a sense of calm in the classes that made them such a pleasure to run. We would have the radio on in the background and often no one would speak for half an hour, everyone was so engrossed in their own work. So, although I was hot, sweaty and exhausted, I was looking forward to an enjoyable evening. Then the phone rang.

'Highgate Pottery,' I answered, assuming already that it was a student ringing to give apologies for tonight's lesson.

'She's dead, you know,' a voice said after a pause. A woman's voice, with an accent, maybe German. It was strangely familiar.

'Who's dead?' Maybe it was a crank call, but I felt a sharp stab of anxiety in my gut. 'Who is this?'

'No. She's definitely dead.'

'Who is this?' I knew I was shouting. 'Who are you?'

'It's Mrs Essenger ... from down the road.'

'Mrs Essenger?'

My brain was fuddled. Mrs Essenger was our neighbour at Walmington Fold, a small bird-like lady with curly hair the texture of boiled wool. She had two boys about my age. We used to ride our bikes together. I hadn't seen any of them, or thought about any of them, for years. She was on the phone, talking. I listened.

My mother had collapsed.

My mother was dead.

I stuck a note on the studio door and jumped in the car. I was back at West Finchley in fifteen minutes.

My mother was *the* stable force through my formative years. She was absolute in the love she bestowed on my sister and me when we were growing up. From my secondary school years, we had bonded over pottery. She had understood I was fascinated by it and had always gone the extra mile to encourage me. When I was fifteen and totally obsessed, we had both enrolled for classes at the local Adult Education Centre. She would go during the day with her best friend Felicity Jordan (my friend Tim's mother) and I would go in the evening, after school. True to her teacher's spirit, she would set herself rigid tasks and diligently worked her way up from the obligatory ashtrays to making a complete set of casserole dishes.

I sprinted down the driveway, around the side and in through the kitchen door. This was where I would usually find my mother bustling around, readying something to eat or drink. Today, she was there, in a way, but it was all wrong. She was sitting on a chair, leaning to one side, her head resting on the fridge door. Entirely still. I called out to her, and as I did, Felicity Jordan came rushing in from the hallway.

'I'm sorry, Keith. I was waiting for you at the front door. I didn't want …'

My mother was completely white; the white only a dead person can be. I had seen it once before, when my grandfather had died. You don't forget it. I looked at her, what had been my mother. I remember thinking she looked fairly pissed off, as if it was all a bit inconvenient and undignified, dying like that, on a chair, leaning against the fridge, wordless.

'I'm so sorry,' said Felicity.

The two of them had been out shopping and my mother – being somewhat overweight – had been struggling with the blistering heat. As they arrived back home she took a turn, as Felicity put it, and went into the kitchen for some water, whereupon she promptly collapsed and died.

Felicity and I shed a lot of tears but exchanged few words. I remember her holding me, like a mother would hold you. She was a large woman, like my mother, and I felt the soft flesh on her shoulders, my fingers pressing into her skin. It was comforting.

The police and the coroner arrived, and all of a sudden the house was full. My father and sister Sarah were still at work, so I was the host. In a weird, auto-pilot daze, I became determined that what we all needed was tea. Yes, tea. Tea would help. I offered everyone tea, and they all said yes. But there was one big problem; my mother, again. The milk was in the fridge, and she was leaning against it. Wordless. White. Dead.

'I know, Felicity! I'll pop across the road to Mrs Johnston.'

Now, Mrs Johnston had lived on our road since the 1950s when the estate had been built, but like Mrs Essenger, I hadn't seen her for years. Without a backwards glance, I dashed over the road and knocked on her door.

'Hello, Mrs Johnston. It's Keith. From across the road.'

Her expression brightened as she realised I didn't want to sell her anything.

'Ooh, what a nice surprise,' she said. 'My, haven't you grown?'

I had – probably two feet since I last saw her.

'Yes! May I bother you for some milk?' She looked mildly surprised. I should have left it at that, but no; I was not in control of my mouth. 'It's really important. You see, my mother has died. And she's in front of the fridge door, and I can't get it open.'

That old chestnut. We stared at each other for a moment.

'You stay there, Keith. I'll go and get you some.' She spoke as if trying to pacify a dog that was about to bite her.

In less than a minute she was back with the milk, handing it over, smiling. I thanked her.

'You take care, Keith. Nice to see you,' she said, closing the door.

Not a word about my mother.

She was only fifty-five.

*   *   *

'Bloody hell,' I remarked to the funeral director, when I went to see my mother in the chapel of rest, 'she looks better dead than she did alive.'

She didn't know how to respond. I tend to look at the humorous side of most situations – it is a coping mechanism, and the only one I had at the time. I was genuinely impressed by the job they had done on my mother, however. She looked well. Her skin was no longer blotchy from the years of sherry drinking and smoking and somehow, she appeared much slimmer in the coffin than she really had been in life. In a peculiar way, the fact that she looked great helped me cope with the funeral.

My sister Sarah took charge of all the arrangements, as my father had shown no interest in doing it himself. He was also skint at the time, so between us, Sarah and I paid for everything. I remember standing outside Hendon Crematorium greeting my friends as they turned up. Each face betrayed genuine shock that I had lost my mother at such an early age. There were lots of hugs but few words. No one knew what to say. The house in Walmington Fold was in no fit state to receive guests afterwards, so we held the wake at the Three Hammers pub in Mill Hill. It was a pretty flat affair; there was no sense that we were there to celebrate my mother's life.

Afterwards, Sarah and her boyfriend Chris invited my father, his sister Brenda, my girlfriend and me back to their flat. No one really wanted to, but a sense of duty compelled us to go. They had not long moved in and had no furniture, so we all sat on the floor in the front room. In silence. Sarah suggested putting on a record that would remind us of Mother. I flicked through her collection, not really knowing what I was looking for, but stopped when I got to 'This Woman's Work' by Kate Bush. It is a powerful song and I knew it would be painful to listen to, but it seemed the right choice.

My father was sitting opposite me. As Kate Bush started to sing, he started sobbing. This was definitely not crying, it was sobbing; sad, gut-wrenching, totally uncontrolled. It was an outpouring of deep-felt emotion, which I had never before seen from my father. Each tear seemed full of regret, as if he was acknowledging that his life would begin to spiral downwards from this moment.

He was sobbing, not only for the loss of his wife, but for *his* part in her death; his long neglect of her pain and depression and his lack of empathy. He was lamenting his failure, sitting cross-legged, utterly broken and ashamed on the floor in a stark, unfurnished room. I remember watching my father and thinking to myself that I never wanted to be his position. He knew he had done precisely nothing to make my mother's life happier or more worthwhile in her final years. Now he had to live with that for the rest of his life – which turned out to be twenty years. I swore to myself that I would never stay in a relationship that was so devoid of love or mutual understanding. I would cry a lot of tears, but never through regret.

It was after the funeral that I began to feel my mother's loss, though for some time I didn't recognise what was happening to me was the result of her death. I started to suffer panic attacks where I would struggle to breathe. Nothing had ever affected me like this before, and I was bemused by how helpless I felt. Within a couple of months, it was taking a toll on every aspect of my life. I was constantly bad-tempered and overwhelmed by a sense of hopelessness.

My way of dealing with it was to stick to my daily routine, only more so, working longer hours. This made me even more irritable. My passion for my craft and hard work was a great help, initially, but no amount of activity can suppress the sort of emotional distress I was experiencing. Finally, I admitted to myself that I needed help. That's when I got in touch with an organisation called Cruse Bereavement.

In my early conversations with my counsellor Jane, I talked about my mother solely from my perspective: she was the trigger that led to discussions of my own issues, and how her death had impacted me. But as the weeks passed and I talked more about my own relationship with her, her own life and her achievements, I started to appreciate, for the first time, that my mother was a person in her own right. It sounds ridiculous, but while alive she had been just 'my mother', and for as long as I could remember, I had only thought about her in that – very selfish – way.

I realised how little I knew about her early life. She rarely spoke about it, and as she had no brothers or sisters, and left no diaries, its mysteries were now lost forever. I do know she was born Keris Margaret Kingsley-Thomas, in Swansea in 1939, and into a relatively well-off family. Her father was a Welsh Methodist deacon, a well-respected and influential man, locally. The family moved to London in about 1950 when Deacon Kingsley-Thomas was offered a ministry there. She attended South Hampstead High, a very good grammar school for girls – or young ladies, rather – where she did very well. As far as I know, everything in the garden was rosy until she was thirteen, at which point her father died quite suddenly.

I recall one story she used to tell about this time. In 1953, Coronation year, my mother's school was chosen to bake one of the tiers for the Coronation cake. It was a great honour and, by all accounts, a great cake. My mother wasn't a royalist as such, but she did have that deep sense of respect for authority that characterised the generation that grew up during the war. She recalled with pride how the whole school went into central London to line the procession route, all wearing their uniforms, including little white gloves. My mother used to pronounce 'white' like the Queen does, making it sound more like 'wheight', which she insisted was the correct way. Maybe she was a bit of a snob in that respect.

She loved reading and cooking – especially baking – and studied hard at school, despite family upheavals due to her father's death. On leaving school at sixteen, she embarked on a domestic science teaching qualification at West Hampstead College, her heart set on teaching children how to cook. When she was halfway through it, her mother was diagnosed with cancer. My mother, still only in her teens, carried on her course while nursing her mother. Sadly, however, within a couple of years she too was dead. When I think about how her own death affected me, I can't conceive how my mother dealt with all this change and shock, emotionally.

She qualified as a teacher and took up a post at John Kelly School in Dollis Hill. By twenty-two, she had met and married my father and the following year my sister was born. At this point she gave up teaching, as was expected in those days of a middle-class woman with a young family. From then onwards, I don't suppose she ever had much time to herself – not until Sarah and I had left home. By then, as I said, she had developed quite a serious drink problem, which I think must have been a result of the depression that seemed to engulf her in the later years of her life.

Her way of coping was to drink. Come five o'clock in the afternoon she would have her first sherry, a Domecq Double Century Amontillado, to be precise, and it would be a large one. She would sit in her chair and as one drink followed another, she would gradually become more and more soaked in bitterness and resentment at how her life had turned out. This bitterness was often directed at my sister. I think my mother was jealous of the freedom Sarah enjoyed, something she never had the chance to experience.

None of this was ever spoken about while she was alive. She, and *we* as a family, simply 'got on with it', as families do. But talking about it during my counselling – her anger, her drinking, her sacrifice – absolutely helped me to come to terms with her loss, and regard her passing in a different, more positive way. I now understood she was still within me and I could still learn from her. I realised how selfless she had been, continuing to offer our family unconditional love and put us first, despite all the suffering and hurt that was buried deep inside her.

It was a lesson learned, and from then on I think I became more empathetic towards the other people in my life. I certainly remember making a conscious decision never to judge anyone on face value again, but to try to see their point of view. It made me accept the probability that most people hold some sort of pain inside them without ever showing it. Certainly my mother did. And by doing nothing to address it, it all became too much for her. There are only so many thermal shocks you can take, before you fall to pieces.

*　　*　　*

The origins of raku are bound up in the tea ceremony. Like the British, the Japanese have always placed great cultural significance around the taking of tea, although for them it's a very formal affair; there's none of your 'quick cuppa'. The tea ceremony lasts for hours, involves a large portion of reflective contemplation and, sadly, no biscuits or cake. Its strict etiquette was defined in the late sixteenth century by Sen Rikyu, tea master to the ruling warlord, Toyotomi Hideyoshi. He applied aspects of Zen Buddhist philosophy and developed Wabi-Cha, a tea ceremony that attached great importance to simplicity, austerity and quiet appreciation. Of course, the tea master needed tea bowls that could embody these values, and tasked his friend Tanaka Chojiro to create them.

Chojiro's bowls were hand-built, then covered in a lead glaze and individually fired at a low temperature. By plucking them from the kiln and letting them cool in the air, he created an oxidation atmosphere whereby the iron and manganese in the glaze reacted with oxygen to produce a matt, citrus skin-like finish. The bowls were monochrome, black or red and without decoration, and they were all tea master Rikyu could have hoped for; a drinking vessel that reflected Zen Buddhism by their imperfection and asymmetry, both fundamentally human qualities.

Chojiro's austere bowls caused a sensation. Considered avant-garde, they were known as *ima-yaki*, which literally translates as 'now ware'. After Chojiro's death, they came to be known as *Juraku* ware, after the area where his pottery was located. This, in time, was shortened to raku. Warlord Hideyoshi was so taken with the new-style tea bowls, he presented a gold seal of approval to Chojiro's son, inscribing it with 楽, the Japanese character for raku. To this day, high quality raku teaware is being produced by the fifteenth generation of the family.

Now here's my final raku fact. When used as a noun in Japanese, the word has a number of meanings, which include: pleasure, ease, content, enjoyment and … felicity! This would have delighted my mother and her best friend Felicity, who enjoyed so many wonderful teas together over the years.

When things were difficult at home, towards the end of her life, I had got into the habit of calling in to see my mother in the afternoon once a week for tea and cake. We would sit with the French doors open looking out into the overgrown green of the garden, chatting over how my business was going, art, politics, what books she was reading … She could read two books a day, and often did. I remember her delight that things were picking up for me. She was proud that I was making a go of things on my own. These are precious memories for me; the two of us talking like two adults, or two friends. And my mother did love a tea party, however small; it gave her the chance to bake.

She would usually bake on a Friday. I would come through the back door and my whole head would fill with the fantastic, warm, luxurious scent of cake. It wouldn't be only one cake, either, she might have ten on the go at one time. These were no ordinary cakes; they were perfectly formed, beautifully decorated and so, so tasty.

Her reason (or excuse) for making so many was because on Saturdays, my father would bring home some of the lads from football, for tea; high tea, to be precise. These men were like kids in a sweet shop when they came in and beheld the spread that had been laid on for them: cream horns, chocolate eclairs, chocolate, lemon and coffee cakes; enough to feed two teams! There were sandwiches too, with the crusts off, but the sarnies were bypassed, always, in the rush to get to the sweet stuff.

When everyone had finished, they would fall into intense discussion of everything and anything, and often the footballing lads wouldn't leave until the early hours of the morning. My mother had a great way of extracting juicy information out of people, usually through the offer of more cake. I would stay up late and take it all in; it was my introduction to how grown-ups talked to each other.

Another speciality was her Christmas cake. It was the same, every year, featuring two ski slopes with snowmen skiing down them through the pine trees. Christmas was big in our house. I remember we always got the biggest turkey possible and we would struggle getting it into and out of the oven. Our decorations would be put in the same place every year, too. There was a tangible sense of reassurance, belonging and comfort in all this; no matter what was happening in the world, all was safe and well in the Brymer Jones household, and it was my mother who brought it together so perfectly.

The first few Christmases after she died were, as you might expect, bloody awful. The tradition that had been present all my life was gone, forever. It's something I miss to this day. And I miss her. Just being here, to be able to sit down with her and have a chat, and a slice or two of cake. Strangely, the last time I got to sample her baking was some weeks after she died. Whenever my mother made a batch of cakes, she would store some in the massive chest freezer in the garage. I was rummaging in there one day, looking for something to eat, and came across this magnificent chocolate cake. It was a real find, a wonderful and a bittersweet surprise. How impatiently I waited for it to thaw.

And how I'd love a slice of that cake with a nice cuppa right now.

12

THE MAD, BAD, NEVER-ENDING 'ISAAC BUTTON' YEARS

If I told you the most expensive hands in the world belonged to a Chinese man, you might well presume he is a potter. Unfortunately, that's not the case. The accolade goes to concert pianist and former child prodigy, Lang Lang, whose priceless mitts are insured for 70 million dollars. Now, that's plain showing off, but I guess it is a wise business move, as without them he'd be up the proverbial without a paddle.

There was a stage in my potting life – a long stage of around fifteen years, in fact – when if I'd had a problem with my hands, it would have been the end of me and my business too. It was back in the days when I made everything – every single piece – by hand, on the wheel at my pottery. Of course, I never insured my hands; I couldn't afford to, but I spent a fortune on hand lotion.

By 1997 Highgate Pottery was turning over £200,000 a year – a lot of money back then. My customer base was growing and those customers could not get enough of my products. The orders kept coming in and those orders kept getting bigger, not that I was complaining, but never mind working 9 to 5, I was working from 5 to 9 to keep it all going, and sometimes even longer. I was thirty then, still fiercely independent and clinging to the belief that long hours and brute force would win the day. If things had to be done, I had to do them, and it was all my responsibility. There was no question of a backward step or easing up; I moved relentlessly towards the very limits of my endurance, my patience, my strength and my sanity. These were the mad, bad, never-ending 'Isaac Button' years.

To give you an idea, they went something like this:

05:00: Up and dressed, bright and early. I never had a problem getting up; my anxiety would come knocking and drag me out of bed. As soon as I opened my eyes, my tasks for the day were right there before me in the front of my mind, forming an orderly queue.

05:10: Out the door. No mucking about with my morning beauty regime. I was living on Finchley Road with my girl-friend and at this hour it was only a twenty-minute drive to Highgate. On the way I would often be treated to the sight of the Royal Horse Artillery taking their horses up to Hampstead Heath for exercise. There would be a whole crowd of them trotting about full of energy, and it always gave me a lift.

05:30: Arrive at workshop, where it would be freezing in winter and boiling in summer. I would put on a big pot of coffee and get to work. I might have any number of orders to prepare or finish, mostly from returning customers. But let's say, on this particular day, I was working on the dreaded Anouska Hempel pots. How I remember those Hempel pots. This order had arrived marked 'urgent' on a day when I already had my tongue hanging out I was so busy. It was from a valuable new customer, an upmarket Notting Hill florist called Woodhams, who had a number of high profile clients.

I couldn't let them down, so I took a deep breath and said I'd squeeze the order in. Initially, they asked for 300 off-white stoneware pots. In each of these would be placed a pure white orchid, and these would then decorate the foyer of the Hempel Hotel, a luxury five-star place near Hyde Park. It was a tight deadline, but the money was good and the pots did not need glazing, which was a bonus. They would need only one firing, which cut production costs and allowed a relatively quick turnaround. In theory.

05:40: Sit down at the wheel. I would have a handful of peaceful hours before anyone else arrived, so I would make the most of them and aim to throw around 300 pieces before things got noisy. The balls of clay would have been prepared the day before by my assistant Simon, so I could just get on with it, working away to the rhythmic whir of my wheel and the restrained chatter of Radio 4.

05:45: Farming Today.

06:00: The *Today* programme. Presented by John Humphrys for over thirty years. In 1997 it would have been him who told me about Dolly the sheep being cloned, or the IBM computer beating Garry Kasparov at chess.

09:00: Maybe next, it would be *In Our Time* with Melvyn Bragg, or perhaps *Desert Island Discs* with Sue Lawley. I didn't go a bundle on *The Moral Maze*, I must admit. Then there would be the distraction of the others beginning to trickle in. I was now employing six staff and basically it was their job to ensure I remained sitting at my wheel, throwing all day. Simon, man of few words but a hard worker, would be at the pugmill, extruding clay and balling it up for me, and I had three full-time packers across the courtyard in the basement of Richardson's, preparing orders for collection or delivery. Then there would be a couple of people who would come in and do odd bits and pieces, sweeping up or fettling (removing excess glaze).

One of these, John, was the sort of Highgate character you saw a lot of in those days, propping up bars in the village, regaling those within earshot in a sonorous, thespian voice. He came from a well-heeled family and didn't have to work – he just needed some beer money. He'd show up in the morning, dishevelled and hungover, but always very charming with it. One day I thought he must have been on a right bender, because he arrived with his jeans on inside out. I let him settle down and have a coffee before mentioning it.

'Ah ... yes. Well,' he said, looking down at the offending garment. 'You see, the other side was quite ... dirty, so I thought I'd sort of ... turn them inside out.'

Another time he was late and I doubt whether the excuse he gave has ever been bettered.

'You'll never guess what happened, Keith …'

A lot of his stories began this way.

'I was in Crouch End and this woman dropped her bag in front of me, so I picked it up and ran after her. As I caught up, she turned round and it was a woman who looked a bit like Chrissie Hynde. She looked at me with her bag and thought I'd stolen it, so she attacked me. She bit me on the shoulder, Keith!'

Did it happen? Well, someone or something did bite John and it was the sort of thing that would happen to him.

09:15: Take a fifteen-minute break from the wheel to have another coffee and go over the tasks for the day with everyone.

09:30: Back on the wheel, and there I would stay until late afternoon, barking out orders every so often. There is no way to rush pottery or cut corners, you have to follow the processes and they take time. One mug might take ten days to complete, for example, start to finish.

With the Hempel pots there were fifteen separate processes involved in bringing them to life, as you can see here:

- First, pugging the clay and preparing it. It would then be weighed and balled up ready for throwing. Simon would generally take around two hours to prepare 300 balls.
- Throwing the pots, as mentioned, usually first thing the next morning. The Hempel pots were fairly straightforward to throw; 10 inches high with a rolled rim. It would take me about three and a half hours to throw 300.

- Next, we put the pots out on the yard wall to dry off a bit. After half an hour they would be dry enough to turn over (though, clearly, not if it was raining, which it did quite a lot).
- Turning the pots onto their rims to let them dry evenly for a further 45 minutes.
- Next, they would need jigsawing and oystering onto long boards. This was about condensing them to fit as many on as possible; the better thrown they were, the more closely you could fit them together. They were then covered with polythene to stabilise the drying process and even out the consistency – like a mini humidifier on the board – and left until the next day. There is nothing like turning pots that have had time to even out properly. It would take about an hour and a half to put all 300 pots onto long boards and lay them out.
- The next day, you would turn them again and leave them for another two and a half hours.
- The Hempel pots had sprigs that needed attaching. These were clay shapes made separately from the main body and applied afterwards. Simon would take about an hour and a half to make the sprigs.
- He would then stick the sprigs onto the pots and stamp them with the appropriate letter, in this case 'H'. This would take about two hours.
- These pots would then be left to dry out for a further two hours.
- Next, someone would have to fettle each pot, which would take about an hour and a half in total.
- Packing the pots into a kiln would take about an hour.
- We would give them a raw firing of 1250 degrees centigrade for twelve hours.

- Then we'd let them cool down for a day and a half.
- Removing them from the kiln would take an hour.
- And then they'd have to be packed.

Phew, eh? And remember, if a pot needed glazing there would be two extra stages. Added to this, the above estimates are 'best case scenario' timings; they don't allow for answering the telephone, making tea, going to the toilet, eating a sandwich, staring into space, nipping down the shops or something going wrong.

Alongside the Hempel pots, on this day we're looking at, I would have larger orders to throw too: 2,000 for Marks & Spencer, 3,000 for Habitat, 1,500 for Monsoon, and so on. If you apply the processes outlined above to these figures, you should get an idea of how challenging, if not relentless, was each day.

Accepting a last-minute order like the Hempel pots was like throwing a spanner into our works, and I remember making them was one of the few times I felt trapped by my work and my commitments. I never thought I would fulfil the order. I never thought I would sleep again. But we got through it, they got made and they looked stunning in the hotel foyer. So stunning that the company kept ordering more. I finished the first batch, by the skin of my teeth, and they asked for another fifty. Then another 100, as soon as possible. It was my own fault; I should have been up front about it and asked them to wait a couple of weeks. But I didn't want to disappoint. In the end we made about 900, but the stress of it made it seem more like 9,000.

Being at the wheel was my default setting between 5 a.m. and 5 p.m. most days, but I would also regularly have to deliver orders up to the Habitat warehouse in Wallingford, near Oxford, which was a 110-mile round trip. Couriers were expensive and I worried they might smash the entire load – worth up to £20,000 for me – so it was less stressful to do it myself. It was relaxing in that I couldn't do anything else but drive and listen to the radio, but in my mind I would be turning over all the things I could have been doing back at the workshop.

15:00: Another reason to abandon the wheel would be a trip to the bank, to pay bills and pay in cheques. On the way back, I would take a few detours to look for waste paper. This was how one-track-minded I was; every moment of every day had to be used wisely with no time wasted. I would regularly drive around Highgate and Crouch End doing a circuit of the paper recycling bins, and you could often find me deep inside one, pulling out all the newspapers so I could shred them and wrap pots in them. I got excited about finding good broadsheets. It was like striking gold, knowing the next Habitat order would be sorted for good-quality, high-brow packaging.

16:00: In the summer, by late afternoon with both kilns going, it would be sweltering in the workshop. I remember one summer I tried out a humidity gauge to measure the moisture in the air and it was 11 per cent – less than in the Sahara Desert! Once I picked up the phone – a big plastic jobby, you remember them – and the receiver was starting to wilt with the heat! To resolve this uncomfortable situation, I put a metal gate on the studio door so I could leave it open at night. It worked, but only up to a point.

If it was a Friday, it would be pay day and I'd walk across the yard to my broom-cupboard office, which generally didn't get that much use. In here were my filing cabinets and my fax machine. Every so often the latter would cough into action and produce something blotchy, but otherwise it was a quiet space. Here I could sit and contemplate while I wrote out cheques totalling about £4,000. I would always wonder if there would be anything left for me at the end of that little routine. Having the kilns going day and night meant my electric bills were astronomical, and then there was the cost of all the clay I needed.

What I was producing was not expensive to buy, considering it was handmade, but cheaper homeware ceramics were starting to appear on the market by then. In 1987, up in Warrington, a Swedish furniture retailer called IKEA had opened up. Ten years later there were a couple of stores in London at Croydon and Wembley. I didn't worry about them too much at this point, as I didn't have the time to stop and consider how they were doing what they were doing, and what it meant for me. But very soon, the way they operated would have a huge impact on my business.

17:00: Simon and the other staff would head off home. I would wave goodbye from my wheel and throw for another hour or so.

18:00: Time to start piling up and covering what was 'going off'. This is a term I used for anything approaching a leather-hard condition. Across the yard were some empty stables that were below ground level. The one right at the end was very damp and perfect for storing pots that needed turning. I could leave them there, then go in the next day and turn them once more to finish off. Board after board would go into this room for turning.

20:00: Finish covering up and putting the pots in the correct area of the pottery for the next day. Often I would prepare handles for the pots I'd been making earlier.

21:00: Start thinking about finishing up for the day. As long as I kept going, my anxiety remained at a manageable level, but if we were *really* busy, there was no way I would be able to go home and relax. So I would keep going, sometimes working until 2 a.m. or later. I once did a 22-hour day, and the buzz I got from that was amazing. After twelve to fourteen hours, you get naturally tired. Then you have a cup of tea, something sweet to eat and carry on. Beyond that you get a weird natural high, almost a state of euphoria. Or maybe it was hysteria.

03:00: Sometimes, I would look at the clock and laugh out loud that I was still working. The yard cat, Hortense, would look at me as if to say, 'Just chill out, will ya, Keith?'

When I did manage to get some sleep, it was comforting to know that my kilns were working for me while I was in the land of nod. The magic that happens when you put a pot through a firing has never ceased to amaze me; as the temperature increases, the molecular structure of the clay changes from a soft organic material you can pull apart to a tough, durable, water-resistant vessel. I would dream about it.

Vitrification occurs at around 1100 degrees centigrade when the last of the water in the clay burns off, as does the sulphur and carbon in it. At that point, the clay particles melt and fuse together and what you have is a ceramic, something that will stick around for a thousand years if you look after it.

05:00: Wake up. What do you know, I'm dressed already! After such a long working day, it would be agony to stand up straight. I visited an osteopath fortnightly to have my back realigned; then I'd undo the work by hunching over my wheel. And so that cycle went round and round.

I guess after reading this you will think I must have been mad to work like this, and you would be right. It impacted every area of my life. But I still loved what I did, even though it was stressing me out 24/7. The ancient Chinese philosopher Lao Tzu said, 'The journey of a thousand miles starts with one step,' and I thought of that every time another humongous order came in. To keep the panic at bay, I used to break down the jobs in my head.

For example, if 3,000 units were required I would break it down in tens like this: $10 \times 10 = 100$; $10 \times 100 = 1000$; $3 \times 1000 = 3000$. Some people count sheep as they're trying to drop off at night, but not me.

I had a warped but very definite sense of pride in my one-man production line. But I was starting to question myself: how long could I keep it up? Would I ever get to see my girlfriend awake again? Would I ever insure my hands?

07:00: Archway Road would start to get busy, the hum steady in the studio. Over the *Today* programme I would hear the cars and buses taking people to where they needed to go to start their day. I would be working the balls of clay that Simon had balled up the previous day and drinking my third cup of coffee.

08:00: Put some more Hempel pots on the wall outside to dry. Dave, the carpenter, would be just opening up.

'Morning, Keith,' he'd say, nodding.

'Morning, Dave,' I'd reply. 'Another day, eh?'

13
HOT

On the night of 9 February 2003, at 11.45 p.m. or thereabouts, my life changed, profoundly and irreversibly. My son Ned was born.

On the days leading up to the big event, however, when my then-wife had to go in for a succession of tests at University College Hospital, I still felt very 'ordinary' and quite detached, in a way. I would wander up and down Tottenham Court Road and then spirit myself into Heals, one of my favourite ever shops (and customers). Absent-mindedly ogling the sofas and soft furnishings, I'd feel pangs of guilt about how totally normal I felt.

I was not burning with anticipation, or physically suffering, or even worrying, really. As the due date came dashing towards us, I felt strangely separate from what was going on back on the ward. The big event was hours away, and yet here I was, calmly stroking a velvet pouffe and drinking coffee.

We had been made aware beforehand that the baby was going to be on the large side, so it was little surprise when they told us he would need to be delivered by C-section. By all accounts, it would be an orderly, 'controlled' procedure, and my first impression on entering the delivery room at the allotted time on the night was the business-like nature of it all. The theatre was incredibly bright, like a motorway service station in the middle of the night, and Radio 2 was droning away on a transistor in the background – like it is when you take your car in to be serviced. But then, a once-in-a-lifetime experience for us was simply another day at work for the excellent midwifery team that helped bring baby Ned into the world.

Don't get me wrong, I'm glad I was present for the birth. I think it's important that fathers are present – if that's what both parents want. However, being a very hands-on kind of person, I found it a bit frustrating standing around without a role, totally useless – maybe as many men imminently about to be fathers feel. The C-section meant I would be even more redundant than most, though, as I wouldn't be able to use the lines 'push, honey, push,' or 'breathe, remember to breathe, go with it'. Maybe that's just as well. For us, the baby was going to be uncere-moniously pulled out like a pair of trainers from a sports bag

– or something. Okay, maybe I *was* getting a little nervous by this time.

Once the epidural kicked in, my wife started to look very considerably woozy and no longer needed or wanted to hold on to my hand. They put a green screen around her midriff. I was advised to stand at my wife's head end, so that I could murmur encouragement, and probably more to the point because apparently men generally faint if they get to see their conscious partner being sliced open. However, I stayed put. You see, I'm curious and not at all squeamish; the opportunity to see inside my partner's body, especially with our baby inside it, was too good to miss.

'Have they started yet?' she slurred, looking a weird combination of both totally relaxed and extremely anxious.

'No,' I lied, staring at whatever part of her anatomy they were currently shifting out of her abdomen – not a baby yet, even I could tell that. 'Everything's fine.'

She was none the wiser as they gathered up what was possibly her stomach and pushed it to one side, although she did tell me she felt a bit sick.

'I'm not surprised, they've just put your stomach on your chest!' I couldn't resist a little joke to lighten the mood. Luckily for me, she didn't remember that later on.

I have to say that by this point in the process, I was pretty wired. I felt full of adrenaline, no doubt the consequence of watching something slightly horrific but also totally awe-inspiring. And then I saw him, curled up among the gore. Yep, our baby was massive. To see this human life in the perfect foetal position, lying within my partner's body, was an amazing sight. I'll never forget the colour of him as he lay there, initially motionless; he was electric blue. Then the midwife yanked him out and smacked his behind, and we heard Ned's first protest against the cruel world:

'I was having a lovely sleep until you went and done that!' – although it sounded more like 'Wahhhhhhhhh!'

'Has he got two arms and legs? Is he all right?' I jabbered, only half joking.

The consultant midwife looked at me like the idiot I so clearly was.

'Nonsense, Mr Jones! He's a perfectly healthy baby boy.'

To add a further surreal touch to proceedings, as Ned cried his little lungs out, the voice of Paul Young could be heard tinnily intoning about leaving his hat at home, or something like that, I'm not sure.

Ned was passed to me, all 11lb 8oz of him (that's almost half a bag of clay!) and for once in my life I was lost for words. I didn't know what to say or feel. I remember thinking how odd it was that this new little person, whom I'd never met before, would be around for the rest of my life.

I held him up to show to his mother. She smiled, then cried, and then threw up a little. As I cradled my son and watched my wife's middle being put back together, I remember thinking that I had definitely got the better end of this deal. But then, suddenly, that was it: I had fifteen more minutes with them both, and then I had to leave. They were taken to the maternity ward, and I was kicked out of the hospital to go home.

It was shortly after midnight and I felt hollow travelling back to Kentish Town on my own. What had just happened? Was it real? In a strange way it felt that nothing had changed, as if I was coming back from the cinema having seen a particularly disturbing horror movie. I didn't feel the fundamental shift that had occurred in my life. But I did feel exhausted.

Once mother and baby returned home a few days later, however, everything changed, of course. Nothing prepares you for all that you have to learn about and deal with in those first few months of a new child's life. Every step felt like a leap of faith. I remember the look of apprehension on Ned's face the first time I changed his nappy. He seemed to sense that I was more worried than him, that I was the novice, the idiot. He was right. We had a tough time as new parents, although probably no worse than most. We both struggled to balance work commitments and child-care and sanity.

Our home situation didn't help matters. We'd moved flats so that Ned could have a room of his own, but the new place in Kentish Town didn't have a lot going for it otherwise. In fact, it was cramped and manky, and what made it worse was that we didn't know anyone in the area, at all. With hindsight, isolating ourselves in that way was a mistake. Not that we had much in the way of family support to call on. Most of my wife's family were up north, and my father hadn't shown the remotest interest in his only grandchild. As for Auntie Brenda, she was still reeling from the shock that babies were born with no teeth.

Then there was my work. I couldn't afford much time away from the pottery as there was nobody else who could step into my shoes and make the pots for me at that time. I felt guilty about it, but there was little I could do other than try to be as supportive as I could when I was at home, and to work my socks off when I wasn't.

The situation was even more ridiculous, because we already had a lovely house that we could (perhaps should) have been living in. You see, by the time Ned was born, we'd been home-owners for four years, but the place we'd bought wasn't in London – we couldn't afford it. Our house was down in

Whitstable, on the north Kent coast. We visited it at odd weekends, and missed it when we weren't there, and it was a daft state of affairs. We were paying a mortgage, plus the rent on the London flat, and could barely afford to live. The problem was, we couldn't – or wouldn't – make that final leap and abandon London for a life on the coast. Personally, I was too firmly entrenched at the Highgate Pottery to consider it.

Having taken so long to get the business established, I'd experienced a downturn in the early noughties and believed a move away at this stage might finish it off completely. It had become impossible to compete with the mass-produced ceramics arriving from all over the world, now on sale in every supermarket and department store. Cheap to buy, the quality was not great, but if they broke you could easily afford to buy another. Suddenly, the emphasis was on piling them high and selling them cheap.

Crazy as it might sound, to stay in the game I was now consciously making my products at a loss. Every order I took, every mug that I threw and fired, I did so knowing I was losing money. It was soul-destroying, yes, but I didn't know what else to do. And borrowing money was easy then; credit card companies were throwing pieces of plastic at you. So I fell back on debt to keep myself in business and put food on the table. It seemed like the only thing to do.

I might well have gone along like this until the bailiffs came to drag me kicking and screaming out of the workshop, had it not been for a fateful meeting with a new buyer from Laura Ashley. Now, new buyers were bad news. The previous one may have thought I was the bee's knees, but a change of personnel usually came with a change in policy; they felt they weren't doing their job if they didn't impose themselves straight away. Often this meant demanding something new from you, something different every season, or other such nonsense. It was a drag continually having to reinvent the wheel for them.

In this case, I had been supplying Laura Ashley for a number of years and had always given them what they wanted. At the time of this visit, my current range was one of the most popular items in the store's interiors department. But I knew tastes were moving away from the quality end of the market, and I knew I could expect no favours based on the past.

The buyer arrived, we exchanged pleasantries and I made her the obligatory cup of herbal tea. By the time I'd returned with it, a stupid smile plastered on my face, she had placed a number of revolting, cheap-looking mugs on my wedging bench. Clearly, she was wasting no time.

'If you can make these for a pound, we can still deal with you.'

There it was, plain, simple, direct. It was impossible to produce a handmade mug for that price. I knew it, she knew it. The mugs would cost me £2.50 to make. There was no other answer I could give but an emphatic no.

'Well, that's it then,' she replied coolly. 'We have no further matters to discuss.'

The tea had barely brewed and the meeting was over. I wondered why she hadn't done this over the phone and saved us both the time.

I'd been in similar situations with other buyers in recent times, but none where the bottom line had been so clear and so … low. I'd said yes to the others, because I couldn't admit to myself that these people were not remotely interested in handmade ceramics, nor the passion, skill and tenacity required to produce large quantities of it. I couldn't accept they were only concerned with hard numbers and units: sell this amount of units for this amount of money and you have a profit. But now, put like this, what else was there to discuss? The situation was suddenly clear as day.

I was badly deflated by the experience, but it was also liberating, in a sense. I knew there was no going back. They say if you know what your weaknesses are, you can overcome them and turn them into strengths. If I had reflected on this at the time, I might well have concluded that I had unwittingly turned one of my strengths into a whopping great weakness: I had placed too much emphasis on my ability to throw large quantities of pots to meet large orders, and kept churning them out, over and over, working and sweating the days away on an ever-shrinking profit margin. It worked when there were three of us throwing at Harefield, but not when it was only me. It wasn't sustainable.

I thought long and hard about what I could do to keep going. In the end, an idea came to me that was so simple, I wondered why I hadn't thought of it before. What I needed was a signature range, something that was mine alone and that would not need changing every few months to keep up with the latest trend. If I was to continue, I had to believe that I was capable of designing and producing a personal range that could stand the test of time, and which people would still want to buy in five, ten or even twenty years.

I got to work. The design I settled on did not take long to come to me. It was influenced, if that is the right word, by my dyslexia – that is, my inability to process words as most readers do. Dyslexia is a commonly accepted learning difficulty these days, but as you know, it made my school life hellish in the seventies. To explain a little: when I see a written word, I don't see the textual information first and foremost, but rather the word's form or shape. I decided to conceive a range of ware that would use words as a design concept.

I had a mug in mind for the prototype, and the inspiration for this was close at hand, or rather, by my feet. Idly looking round the room trying to think of a new, distinctive shape, my eyes fell on the slop bucket that collected water from my wheel tray. The dimensions and proportions were perfect, I thought, and that is how my 'bucket mug' was born. I made it in white porcelain, very simple and understated, and then stamped a single coloured word onto it. I chose the word 'hot', for no other reason than, to me, it just looked right. The link with hot drinks, or any other kind of 'hot' (raises eyebrow seductively), was a happy coincidence.

For the font, I definitely wanted something that looked neat and compact. In research, I struggled to find exactly what I was after, but then it hit me: it should be typed, like on an old type-writer. That's how I settled on using Courier New, and I was really pleased with the result. It looked like something that had been around for ages, and where the words were concerned, the possibilities were literally endless.

I found this old printing firm in the East End that did type-setting for newspapers, a real traditional printers with old presses and everything. They could create these zinc plates for any word I wanted. I would send them artwork at 3 p.m. and, because they worked through the night, would later drive down there around 2 a.m. to pick up the finished piece of work. I would usually pop into the all-night bagel shop on Brick Lane on the way back, which was always a big treat for me.

It very quickly became apparent that people liked the 'Word Range', as I called it. Heals, one of my oldest customers and favourite pre-baby haunts, picked it up first, and it was soon flying off the shelves. Other customers reported the same. When I took it to a trade fair not long after Ned was born, I took

£35,000 worth of orders. It was then that I knew I was on to something. At the very least, it would keep a few debtors off my back.

*　　*　　*

I had 'discovered' Whitstable way back in the days when I was delivering parcels for Abis Brand Couriers. Every now and then, breaking up the monotony of crawling through hours of London traffic, you'd be given an out-of-town job. One happy Friday afternoon I found myself driving down the A2 to this sleepy-cum-rough-around-the-edges harbour town. It appealed to me straight away, both with its air of a bygone, industrial past and with its feeling of space and air that I gorge on when I'm close to the sea. It became a favourite getaway spot for my girlfriend and me. None of our London friends had heard of the place, so it was our little secret, somewhere we could forget about our stressful London life and relax.

Soon after we were married, we decided Whitstable would be the perfect place to buy a house, mainly because we didn't have a hope in hell of ever buying one in London. But when we bought, we weren't quite ready for 'settling down' and having babies. In fact, very few of our friends had become parents. It simply wasn't the done thing. Our generation was eschewing the responsibility of kids for as long as possible, extending our adolescence into our mid-thirties – although I think it was as much a financial choice as a lifestyle one. However, as the millennium approached, couple by couple started to succumb. There was a spate of weddings, as we finally realised there was more to life than having a good time, all the time.

That we could afford a mortgage on a house at all was a triumph in our eyes. The one we ended up buying in Whitstable

cost less than a pokey two-bedroom flat in an unfashionable part of London. Situated on a road leading down to the beach, it was perfect for us. It made us laugh how much room we had, after having to squeeze everything into a tiny flat for years. Being by the sea, it felt as if we were always on holiday there, and we had a steady flow of visitors coming down from London to spend the weekend with us. Within a few years, some of our closest friends took the plunge and also moved down to take up residence (and jobs) in and around Whitstable, including my old bandmate Mick.

On finally deciding to leave London, I mused over the words of Dr Johnson (no, really – I did!), who famously put it to his biographer James Boswell that, 'When a man is tired of London, he is tired of life; for there is in London all that life can afford.' Earlier in my life, I'd have heartily agreed with him on this. In fact, I could never have imagined living anywhere else, because I didn't think there could be anywhere better. Now, pushing forty, skint and knackered, I thought it was a load of old tosh. What did Dr Johnson know, anyway? And why should I take any notice of a man who spent eight years writing a dictionary, a thing that is every dyslexic's worst nightmare?

Ned's birth had indeed changed everything. Keeping up two homes was never going to be possible in the long term, and the constant juggling, going back and forth between Kent and London, was emotionally and physically wearing, too. As other friends were now living down in Whitstable, my wife and baby Ned started staying down there more frequently. The flat in Kentish Town became unloved, and then redundant. We gave it up.

But despite moving all our possessions down to the coast, I was still stubbornly hanging on to the Highgate Pottery, and for a mad period I was commuting up to town on a Monday and then staying up for most of the week, sleeping on a tiny camp bed in my little office and eating pitta bread and dips for dinner, meanwhile missing my baby son. One morning, after I'd spent half an hour trying to straighten out my seized-up back, I thought to myself – enough is enough.

What I'd always dreaded was moving the pottery itself. I had promised my wife I would complete the move before Ned's second birthday, but with the clock ticking, I was struggling to find anywhere suitable. Then I had one of those pieces of good fortune that have happily seemed to present themselves at key moments in my life. I don't usually take notice of advertisement cards in newsagents' windows, but one afternoon in the High Street, Whitstable, I saw a card advertising a cheap studio space.

Now, Whitstable is a small town, so I recrossed the road and headed straight for the given address. It was on a side street, a building with an impressive frontage that had once been a bakery. I knocked at the grubby wooden door. After a short wait, it was answered by a scruffy man who clearly liked to leave long gaps between haircuts and beard trims.

'Yes?'

He was very well-spoken, though. He collected junk, from what I could gather from his brief snatches of conversation. From what I could see, it was not making him much of a living.

But his building was perfect for me: a large airy space on two floors with a mezzanine on the second floor. The ground floor was where the bakery ovens had been. Once cleared of scrap, there would be plenty of room for all my equipment, plus a spacious office and lots of storage room. There was even a loading bay door on the first floor.

'When can you clear the place?' I asked, already working out where I could put everything.

'Oh no,' he replied. 'You can't have the whole place. I was thinking half the downstairs area.'

I told him that was no use to me and that I wasn't interested. He then said he could stretch to the whole of the downstairs, but he was very vague about when the place would be available.

'Ooh, well, I'll have to shift this lot,' he said, eyes gleaming sadly.

I could tell there was no way on earth *he* was going to shift anything. I left, thinking it would never come to anything, but he got back to me soon after with an offer. First of all, he admitted that it wasn't his property (as I had suspected), but he said he would be willing to sublet me the entire downstairs space.

'If you can pay the rent before Christmas, it's yours,' he told me.

This was December 2004. Ned's second birthday was six weeks away, and mindful of my promise, I agreed to his proposal. The day I went round to pick up the keys, our junk collector was really on edge and the downstairs was still a right old mess, as I'd expected. He handed me the keys and some contact details, which I quickly noticed weren't his. As I tried to clarify the new arrangement he was edging towards the door, and before I could finish, he piped a quick 'goodbye for now' and was gone. I never saw him again.

A week or so later, I telephoned the number he'd given me, which I assumed must belong to the real landlord. I was correct, and he seemed relieved to be rid of his former tenant when I explained the situation. He told me he'd be down to see me in the New Year. That didn't give me long to sort the place out, and now I was in, I was determined to hold on to the place. I knew I'd have to get the pottery fully set up before the visit took place, so it would be difficult for him to chuck me out if he did not approve.

I moved the pottery from Highgate to Whitstable almost entirely under my own steam, and it nearly killed me. The nervous and physical energy I expended left me hyper-stressed and dehydrated and I even experienced an attack of gout. Gout!! Gout is something only port-drinking, duck-guzzling old men get! The pain was like nothing I've ever experienced. Once I'd finished unloading the van, I could barely walk. I was virtually bent double and limping like mad Igor out of the old Frankenstein films. It's lucky nobody saw me; I'd have scared them half to death.

I needn't have worried about my new landlord. When he finally did visit, a couple of months later, I was up and running and he was delighted the place was being properly used.

'Cor blimey,' he said, looking the place up and down. 'You've done more in a couple of months than has happened in fifteen years to this place.'

He said I could have the lease for as long as I wanted. I almost jumped up and down. I may have cried.

And so we began a new life in Whitstable. It was an ideal environment to bring up our son, and for me it was a more relaxing place to live. Instead of finishing work and having to deal with London's traffic maelstrom, I could ease into the laid-back pace of the town. Ned was now a toddler and a bubbly, chatty little character, and I now had time I could spend with him instead of being exhausted every day. I got to experience all that was wonderful and special about being a parent: teaching my son new things, playing with him, watching him grow up.

Being an Aquarian, Ned loved the sea. We couldn't keep him away from it. Some parents get very nervous about their children being around water and I was a bit like that, at first. Then one afternoon I was in the sea mucking about with Ned and my mate Mick. Ned was splashing around in his little dinghy happily enough, so Mick and I got chatting. Thirty seconds later, I looked around and the dinghy was empty. My heart turned over as I saw Ned's checked shirt disappearing beneath the waves. I dived over and hauled him up to the surface, expecting him to be coughing water and crying. But he was fine; he was beaming. He loved it! After that I knew I needn't worry about him.

He'd often look up at me with the same look he gave me that day. Looking at his dad. Me. It always made me acutely aware of that bond between us, that look. *Those* are special moments.

14

'YOU DO THE POTS AND I DO THE PENNIES'

Queen Victoria's consort, Prince Albert of Saxe-Coburg and Gotha, was not a royal who wasted his time opening garden fêtes. He was an all-round, can-do geezer, designing grand houses like Osborne on the Isle of Wight, taking interest in the arts and sciences, and supporting educational reform and the abolition of slavery. If you are somebody who likes to get things done, it does help if your other half is Queen of the world's largest empire and totally minted.

So when Albert decided to stage the Great Exhibition in 1851, which was essentially the world's first trade fair, he was going to do it in style. Even the building they hosted it in, the beautiful and sadly lost Crystal Palace, was a wonder of British engineering, being constructed using 293,000 panes of glass, and including the largest sheet glass ever made up to that point.

Of course, carting goods along to sell at some central place has been practised weekly in British market towns for centuries, and long before that there were the Middle Eastern bazaars established along ancient trade routes such as the Silk Road.

Today, as you might expect, there are trade fairs dedicated to almost every possible product there is. In the commercial construction industry, 'The World of Concrete' is one of the biggest attended shows in the world. If that sounds a bit dry, how about the 'Annual Psychic Fair and Witchcraft Expo', which takes place in Salem, USA? Or for bird-lovers there is 'Deutsche Junggeflügelschau', which translates as the German Young Poultry Show. With over 11,000 chickens, geese, and ducks on show, that probably ranks as one of the foulest-smelling shows around, pardon the pun.

For me, trade fairs became a necessity back in the mid-1990s when I was trying to reach more buyers. Before the internet, there was no better way to raise awareness of what you had to offer. But it was expensive: a modest stand of 3m x 3m would cost me around £4,000. The thing was, I invariably made my money back. Another thing about trade fairs is that they involve an arse-numbing amount of sitting around waiting. Waiting to set up, waiting to open, waiting for someone to approach, stop in their tracks at the sight of my lovely pots and mugs and say, 'Hey, these are great! I'll take five thousand.'

Needless to say, that didn't happen too often. Usually, people would shuffle up and glance surreptitiously at something, then check the price. I found that if I tried to engage them in conversation, it would scare them off and they'd move on to the next stand. So I learned to stay put and let them browse; if they were genuinely interested, they would come and speak to me.

I was a trade fair veteran of some ten years by the time I attended an event at London's Olympia Exhibition Centre in 2006. Things were ticking along nicely, as my Word Range was proving a good seller and I was on course to turn a tidy profit. Being up in London also gave me the chance to catch up with old friends in the evenings, so I might well have been musing on where to go later when an unassuming punter strolled over to my stand. I adopted my default, nonchalant attitude and we exchanged milky smiles.

My first impression was that he looked unremarkable, another bloke in expensive jeans and a polo shirt. I waited for him to shuffle off, like so many others. But he didn't. He came over and spoke to me.

'Hello! I'm Dom,' he said.

He was well-spoken; think Prince William but posher. In fact, he didn't look too dissimilar to the heir to the throne. I guess that helped get my attention. He didn't waste any time in getting to the point.

'I really like your pots,' he said, indicating my Word products. 'They're the best thing I've seen here.'

He said this with a kind of child-like candour, which made me believe he really meant it.

I thanked him for his compliment and asked if he had a shop or store. He said he didn't and explained that he'd been looking at my work for some time and wondered if I was interested in getting it mass-produced.

'I think we could scale it up,' he told me.

I couldn't believe my ears. I was irritated. What did he mean by 'we'? But he didn't stop there.

'I've been looking for someone like you for a long time. If you wouldn't mind, could I take a piece away with me and get it produced in a factory, so that you can see what you think?'

As a business proposition, it must have broken some sort of record. I had not met him five minutes ago. I still wasn't sure what he was: a manufacturer? Minor royalty? An imposter? A con man? A madman? He sensed my unease and turned to look at my display as I stood there dumbly, grinning and frowning, wondering what had hit me.

'Look, Keith,' he said, obviously deciding to go all-in with my forename. 'I've got no design sense and quite frankly, I'm colour blind. But how about you do the pots and I do the pennies?'

It was a simple, unsubtle approach, I had to give him that. But I liked him straight away because of it. I gave him one of my bucket mugs and he said he'd be in touch. Did I think he could come back to me with a factory product that emulated my handmade one? Absolutely not. But I admired his openness and honesty, and … what did I have to lose? It was only a mug after all.

Some weeks passed and I didn't hear anything, but I couldn't help thinking about what Dom had said about 'scaling up' the Word Range. I'd already been in talks with another company, in Birmingham, about doing exactly that, but the samples they had sent back to me just didn't look like my work. That experience had made me doubt that Dom would be able to achieve any better.

I was busy making an order from the Olympia Trade Fair when Dom finally called me back. He'd got the mug back from a factory in China and wanted to show it to me. I told him to pop over sometime, in an off-hand kind of way.

'How about I come and see you now?' he said, forcing the issue. I was snowed under and reluctant to drop everything immediately. But I was too intrigued to say no.

I was putting some pots out to dry when he breezed in, holding a small box. He walked up to me, opened it, and pulled out a white porcelain mug. I took it from him and turned it over and over in my hands.

It was good. Very good, in fact. The clay itself was porcelain, a smoother, creamier white finish than mine was, but the quality was excellent. It glistened in the sunlight that poured into the yard. The light hit the surface of the glaze like a diamond sparkling in a jeweller's shop window. The dimensions were exact and the stamping of the word 'Love' on it was incredible. Looking at my own creation in this context was strange; like I was looking at it anew. I realised how my decision to use Courier font had really enhanced the design. It looked as if it had been typed, exactly the effect I'd wanted.

Every day I count my blessings that Courier is in the public domain and there is no copyright to prevent me using it. The typeface was designed in 1955 by Howard 'Bud' Kettler for the American computer company IBM. Initially it was for use with their typewriters, but has since been adopted across the globe, notably as a standard font for computers. It is monospaced, meaning all the characters are the same width, so for example, an 'i' receives as much room as a 'b', even though it is thinner. Originally it was called Messenger, but Kettler renamed it because, as he put it, 'a letter can be just an ordinary messenger, or it can be the courier, which radiates dignity, prestige, and stability'. I like that. The font undeniably contributed to the mug's aesthetic appeal and Dom's factory-made version had definitely captured that.

At this point I had mixed emotions; on the one hand, I was impressed by the quality of the mug and the thought that had gone into replicating my original. On the other, I was apprehensive about the new path that had opened up ahead of me. Not a path, it was way more than that – more a motorway. I could already see that it was totally unavoidable. If my business was to survive, and if I was to continue being a potter, I would have to go into partnership with a stranger and start on mass production.

Dominic Speelman is ten years younger than me. He had what I would consider a privileged upbringing, attending St Paul's School, which is one of the country's top independents – a notch or two above St Mary's, Hendon, for sure. He was still in his twenties when he recognised what China had to offer by way of business opportunities. He learned to speak Mandarin – no mean feat – and set up a viable business structure with an office in Hong Kong and links with suppliers and manufacturers on the Chinese mainland.

By the time we met, when he was in his early thirties, Dom had enjoyed some success with a venture called, wait for it, 'Same but Cheaper'! An awful name and concept, in my opinion, but you couldn't argue with what he'd achieved. What he had lacked up to now was a decent product. That's where I came in. With a much better business name. Together, we would be Make International.

★   ★   ★

It is strange when I think back to those early years of Make International, how the pattern of my working day changed so completely almost overnight. Now I was not sitting at my wheel churning out pots from dawn till dusk; that was being done in a factory in China. I was spending more time designing as we were constantly looking to expand our range, and I was travelling a lot, going over to China four or five times a year. Bad for the planet, but what an experience.

We were also attending a lot of trade fairs. The need to be noticed at these was paramount, so there would be no more of the tiny stands like the ones I used to man all on my lonesome. The stands and displays got bigger as our company grew. I would design them and they'd be custom built, bit by bit, by Dom's cousin Russ. They were major construction jobs and meant we'd now have to arrive at an event a day early to put them together, and allow a day afterwards to take them back down.

One of the first shows we did with a scaled-up display was at the Birmingham NEC Trade show. It cost us £30,000. Prior to this, Dom and I had tended not to discuss the money side of things so much. But this bigger initial outlay meant we both felt a shift in what was at stake. For this show, we had hired a small cottage to stay in for the duration of the event and as we left one morning, Dom turned to me and asked how committed I was to Make International, seeing as we didn't have a formal agreement. I was surprised at the way he brought this up, just after breakfast and all, but I could see what he was getting at.

'It's like this, Dom,' I told him. 'I want to go anywhere in the world and be in a hotel, restaurant, or even someone's house, and I want to turn the plate, mug, or bowl over and for it to say "Make International" or "KBJ". And until that happens, I ain't stopping.'

His reaction was priceless.

'Oh. Okay, then,' he said, and we toddled off to the NEC.

It may have been naïve, but we both had the same dream. And this being the case, we had total trust in each other's resolve.

Going abroad to do a trade fair has been good fun with the Make International team. The days are long and you are on your feet the whole time, yakking to customers or other delegates. Then in the evening, the serious business begins: deciding where to go and eat. Dom is always keen to seek out the very best places and we've had some memorable nights out. Come to think of it, the mornings haven't been too bad either.

One place I really loved was Yolk in Chicago, where we ate every morning before the Housewares show there. It's such a fun-looking place with its blue, white and yellow interior, and I promise you, the breakfasts are quite simply gargantuan. A cooked breakfast is definitely my kind of meal; a good one is as good as eating gets, in my book.

Chicago is also the coldest place I have ever been. With the wind coming off Lake Michigan, the temperatures would plummet to minus 20°C, which is far too low for the likes of me. I thought I was a goner there one time. At the end of an exhausting day setting up our stand, Russ and I, all hot and bothered, decided to walk back to our hotel. The moment we stepped outside, we knew we'd made a terrible mistake. I thought my sweat would freeze and deposit tiny ice-cubes down my sleeves.

I looked round at Russ, who must have rued the day he decided to shave his hair off, because his head was turning pale blue. He told me mine was, too. So we had a little competition going: 'Who has the bluest head?' and that kept us occupied, sort of, until we gratefully pushed open the door of our hotel. The feeling was amazing. Luckily, we had thawed out nicely in time for dinner.

As ever, with the trade fairs I do tend to want to be in control of things, down to the last little detail. Just as back in the day at Highgate Pottery, when I would sit at my wheel directing proceedings, I feel myself getting stressed if everything is not going along like clockwork. It's a trait I wish I didn't have, but I do. I guess it's my OCD. If something is not 'just so', it sends me out of kilter. This can have undesirable consequences.

One time Russ, Marj and I were loading up a Luton Van ready to drive over to Paris for the *Maison & Objet* trade fair. I love Paris and this was going to be Marj's first ever visit, so I was looking forward to showing her around. The van was jam-packed. We should have got a bigger one, but we were trying to save money. We were also on a tight schedule, and with time running out to catch our train on Eurotunnel, I suddenly remembered that we still had to pick up a strip of aluminium floor cornicing for our stand.

There's nothing like a clock ticking to raise a sweat on my brow and a skip in my heartbeat. We pulled up outside the sheet-metal suppliers with a squeal of tyres. The bloke in the shop knew we were in a hurry and was ready with our aluminium. I jumped out and opened up the back of the van for him. He hesitated.

'Oi, mate, do you need me to cut it down?' he asked. 'It doesn't look like it'll fit. It's too long.'

'No, it's fine, lovey,' I assured him. 'I'm sure it's okay. I'm sure.'

I was certain, in fact, having measured it precisely myself: it would fit with two inches to spare. He looked doubtful and indeed, when he tried to feed it in, there was still a bit poking out. I jumped up onto the van floor and then over a pallet to try to make room and slide the metal in myself. What I had not considered was that I was far too tall for this type of jumping manoeuvre in the van. I felt a rush of cold pain and then a warm sensation. I looked up to see what had caused this. There was some sharp metal flashing running along the centre of the van roof and I'd scraped my head on it, effectively scalping myself.

As I staggered out, blood gushing everywhere, the man holding my aluminium went white as a sheet. I tore off my white linen shirt, mindful not to ruin it (I didn't!), and then rushed round to the front of the van. Marj and Russ were excitedly discussing where we might go on our first night in Paris, when this character out of the *Texas Chainsaw Massacre* appeared before them. Realising it was me, they jumped out and gawped at me, horror etched across their faces.

The shop let me in to use their bathroom and once we'd got my head under some running water, Marj was able to make a diagnosis.

'Part of your scalp is a bit flappy,' she told me.

Flappy didn't sound good. Flappy sounded like hospital. We couldn't go there, we had a Eurotunnel train to catch. My mind briefly weighed up the alternatives; should I buy a hat, or seeing as we were bound for France, a beret, perhaps? The blood cascading down my forehead and bare chest made the decision for us all, so we jumped in the van and sped off to Canterbury Hospital A&E department, which luckily was close by. By some miracle, I was seen straight away and a nurse set to work on stapling and gluing my scalp back onto my skull.

'How does it look?' I asked, as the nurse squeezed out the last globule from the second tube of glue.

Marj gave me a thumbs up. I knew she was taking the piss, but I didn't care; all I could think about was catching that train. The nurse took my blood pressure and did a double take when she looked at the reading.

'Oh! This is bad,' she said, suddenly quite concerned. 'Your blood pressure is high. Really high. I can't let you go until it's much lower.'

Obviously, those words sent my pressure way higher.

'He'll be fine,' Marj said. 'He's always like this.'

The nurse raised an eyebrow; surely if I was always 'like this', I should be dead!

Marj gamely fought my corner. I certainly couldn't. Finally, the nurse relented and said I could go. We made a dash for the van, Russ put his foot down and we made it to our train on time. I have to say, I wasn't on top form at dinner that evening and felt pretty woozy for a few days, but I survived. Oh, and by the way, the aluminium strip did fit in the back of the van, after all.

Believe it or not, these first few years of my partnership with Dom were completely based on trust. Nothing was signed, in fact nothing at all was agreed in writing. All that existed was that initial first 'pots and pennies' understanding. There was a connection between the two of us from the start, but it took me some time to pinpoint exactly what that was. It dawned on me one morning when Dom was talking about his father, a very successful businessman. It seemed to me he was driven by a need to prove himself to his father, to be a success on his own terms. I felt that need, too. Only I wanted to prove it to myself.

When I first clapped eyes on Dom, he didn't look like someone who was about to set my life on a new course. I don't suppose I did to him, either. But in each other, we both found something we'd been looking for, a piece of the puzzle that was missing. Maybe it's fate.

Perhaps, if we'd been born 2,000 years ago, we'd have bumped into each other somewhere along the Silk Road, him in his sensible shoes and me limping from some recent mishap. I'd be sat at a table with a monster bowl of dates and figs before me, breakfasting like a king.

He'd sidle up to me and say: 'I like your pots.'

15

BIG FAT, WHITE
HAIRY GORILLA

I opened my eyes a little after 7 a.m. on my first morning in Hong Kong, got out of bed and crossed the floor to the window. Thirty-one floors below, Hong Kong was already wide awake and a great hubbub was rising up from the streets. Although I badly wanted to go down and join in with it, there was something I had to do first. Five minutes later, I was three floors up, swimming across the roof with a great big grin on my face. It was one of those infinity pools.

If I squinted, the tugboats chugging across the harbour looked like they were in the deep end waiting for me to swim over and sink them. Far below in Victoria Park, I could make out great swathes of synchronised humanity going through their fan dance and tai chi routines. High above, eagles were flying about observing all this and more. Eagles! Before breakfast! There have been some moments during my life, not many, when I have looked skyward and thought to myself, how did I end up here? This was one of them.

In keeping with the spirit of our whirlwind business partnership, Dom had flown me over to the gateway to China to visit the Hong Kong office and set up some meetings with factories on the mainland. When we arrived at our very plush hotel, I strained my neck trying to see the top of it. The doorman recognised Dom.

'Good evening, Mr Speelman,' he said. 'Nice to see you again.'

I was impressed, though less so when I found out we had to share a double bed to save some money. It was my first trip outside Europe or the States and my first experience of a totally different culture. But that first night we sat on that bed and mapped out our plans for world domination, putting a big dent in our mini-bar in the process.

The following day, after my high-flying morning dip, Dom took me to our office to meet Stephen and his nephew, Terence, who ran our business operations there. It was strange for me to think of this office as mine. It was on the 33rd floor with the obligatory panoramic view of the city that I would soon come to take for granted. I thought of the windowless cupboard across the yard at Highgate Pottery where I used to go through my invoices, write cheques (remember those?) and wait for my fax machine to whir out another order. Blimey!

Stephen and Terence were Hong Kong Chinese and no, that wasn't what they were really called. When working with Western companies, locals often adopt a Western name. Apparently, they first do this when they are taking English lessons, as it's easier for the teacher to remember them. Whatever the reason, it certainly saves time on pronunciation. Perhaps I should reciprocate and adopt a Chinese name when I'm over there. I wonder what the Mandarin for Potman is?

Stephen, being the elder, was very traditional Hong Kong in his outlook. He still identified more with the British than the Chinese, tended to look down on the Chinese, and was paranoid in any dealings with the mainland. His attitude was deep-rooted, harking back to the city's colonial past, which of course only ended in 1997. On the other hand, he was very well intentioned and there was nothing he wouldn't do for you, whether it was part of his remit or not. Terence, being younger, wasn't influenced by the old days. During that first trip, I saw that he was a highly skilled graphic designer and I subsequently developed a strong relationship with him, based around our creative output.

I had never experienced anything like Hong Kong. I couldn't understand a word of the language, so I followed Dom and Stephen around like a lost schoolboy. The main reason for our visit was to visit factories we could partner with and which would potentially manufacture our pots. We were looking for the perfect blend of price and quality and knew that wouldn't be easy to find. We visited six or seven times that first year and saw about twenty-five factories, all in the area around the city of Chaozhou, which is China's Stoke-on-Trent. Literally mountains of domestic ware are produced in this region.

In 2004, central Chinese government officials awarded it the title 'porcelain capital' in recognition of the size, volume and output of its porcelain manufacturing. By 2011, its production value was worth nearly $8 billion. That's quite a lot.

Stephen liked to talk, and my overriding memories of our first tour of the factories are of listening to his voice. Dom could speak Mandarin, but there are countless local dialects that are impenetrable to the outsider. Often, we'd both be standing there, none the wiser about what was being said. Sometimes I got the gist of it, but more often I'd be way off mark. The Chinese tone can often seem aggressive (though you could say the same of many British accents). Sometimes I got the impression that Stephen might be about to lamp the factory owner, when all they were talking about was the price of a mug.

To be honest, I was extremely sceptical going out there. I didn't think we'd find somewhere that could reproduce what I made, satisfactorily. To an extent I was simply enjoying the ride. That perception gradually altered as we toured the factories. Because of Stephen and Terence's connections, we were getting to see the ones that other Western companies would not have done. They were family-run businesses that had been handed down from generation to generation and ceramics was like a religion to them. It was in their blood.

I was really nervous going into the first factory. Because I was stepping into the unknown, for some reason, I didn't think that I would recognise any of the machinery, or even the processes taking place. I thought the Chinese would see me as an imposter, like I knew nothing. As I'd expected, it was buzzing with activity. To my great relief, the machinery I saw made me feel right at home: the ware trolleys, the jiggers, the pugmills, the batting out machines; much of it had been made in Stoke-on-Trent and all was painted in the familiar metallic green or blue paint.

I remember being puzzled by the colourful, highly decorated dresses worn by the female workforce. They looked as if they were going out for the evening, in contrast to the men in their T-shirts and shorts. I would find out this was very normal, as Chinese women like to dress nicely to go to work. That seemed to be the only real significant difference from the factories back home.

Everywhere we visited, we took samples of my pottery and that would form the basis of our test for each factory: I wanted to know exactly how they would go about replicating my pots. Dom wanted to know what the cost would be. It wasn't always easy from my point of view, as they were not going to let some English bloke poke his nose around their factory. I knew I had to bide my time and wait for them to invite me into their world.

One aspect I had no worries about was the raw material all the factories were using. It was second to none. Furthermore, kaolin (china clay) was abundant in this region of south-eastern China and most factories had their own quarry, essentially giving them access to free, high-quality clay.

The Chinese have been making porcelain, known as hard-paste, since the Yuan dynasty (1279–1368). Particular skill and patience is required to make it: no other ceramic is as thin, as durable or as delicate and luminous. These qualities helped to make it extremely popular following its introduction to Europe by Portuguese traders in the sixteenth century. It helped that Europeans were becoming addicted to tea around the same time, as wealthy families would spend a great deal to outdo their neighbours and have the best quality porcelain tea sets to show off.

Until the eighteenth century, porcelain's formula was a secret outside China. European potters and manufacturers were frantic to discover it and to produce their own ceramics and cut in on what was a huge global market. The man credited with making the breakthrough was German alchemist Johann Friedrich Böttger, whose experiments with kaolin led to the Meissen factory near Dresden being the first to make its own porcelain in 1710. Ten years later, it was so popular that they incorporated a logo onto their ware to deter copyists. Their 'crossed swords' logo was one of the earliest known trademarks.

Meissen was not forthcoming in sharing the secret either, but by now it was common knowledge that kaolin was a key ingredient. In Britain, William Cookworthy, a Quaker chemist, was set on going one step further than Böttger. He not only wanted to discover how to make hard-paste porcelain, but he was determined to source his own supply of kaolin as well. In 1845, he started travelling from his home in Plymouth around the west of England, searching for the elusive mineral. It took him a year, but he hit the jackpot, discovering the white gold at Tregonning Hill in Cornwall.

What he had unearthed was indeed similar to Chinese kaolin, but coarser, and it had to undergo a process of refining to make it usable. It took him over twenty years of experimenting to perfect this and he didn't get to patent it until 1768, by which time better quality kaolin had been found at nearby St Austell – and in huge quantities. Cookworthy may have been the first man in Britain to make hard-paste porcelain, but he didn't profit by it, and by 1774 he had sold his interest in the business.

A great industry developed around the enormous open-cast St Austell mines and it's one that is still going strong. The porcelain I buy from Stoke-on-Trent is sourced from there. It is very good, but still not of the standard of that found in China, and the reason for this is a vital missing ingredient: petuntse. This feldspathic rock, when ground to a powder and added to kaolin clay, allows it to be fired only once, at high temperature, about 1450 °C (2650 °F). It is what gives porcelain its durability and glass-like consistency. Petuntse means 'little white bricks', a reference to the way it was originally divided up and sent out to factories. You don't get this in Britain, and it makes a huge difference.

Despite being impressed by what I saw in the Chinese factories, deep down I still wanted to use one back home to manufacture my pots, preferably in Stoke-on-Trent. The problem was, Dom and I wanted to keep our products affordable, and however we did the maths, making them in Britain would mean pricing them higher and making them luxury items rather than everyday ware. After many years of not making much financially from my work, this opportunity was too good to pass up. In China, we didn't have to buy clay and everything would require only one firing. It was a no-brainer.

*   *   *

One of the factories we ended up taking on as a partner was run by two brothers, Ben Zhang and Yi Zhang. Ben Zhang ran the business side of things and looked like something out of a 1970s gangster film, with his shiny two-tone suit and the long French cigarettes he chain-smoked. I think he considered himself very much what the British in the 1950s would have referred to as 'a ladies' man'. I liked him instantly, but I didn't think I would ever be able to trust him, as there was something of the lovable rogue about him.

His brother, Yi Zhang, was a far less complex character and much more practical and down to earth. He ran the production side. He made a bit of a song and a dance about things we asked him to do regarding my pots, and he seemed to find a problem in everything he did. Maybe it was because he was a perfectionist; he always came up with a solution, and his finished product was stunning in its quality. Every piece he brought back to show me was on the money.

Yi Zhang's affinity with clay was clear to me. When I handed him a sample of mine, it was like I was passing him a precious relic. He didn't see it, he *felt* it. Checking its thickness, its weight, its volume and its definition. I felt that familiar tidal wave of emotion hit me as I watched him assess my pottery. It was like the entire history of Chinese porcelain manufacturing was concentrated into his fingers. For me, it was a pivotal moment and I knew that this was the factory we'd been looking for.

I wanted to go on to the factory floor to see the workers and maybe do some throwing. Ben Zhang was perplexed by my request, as he couldn't understand why I would want to. Now, he had one very long nail on the little finger of his right hand and I was intrigued to find out it signified that he didn't do manual work, because it was beneath him. Stephen explained to him that I came from a pottery background and that I didn't mind getting my hands dirty. In fact, I preferred it. It was a cultural difference that neither of us understood, but we met in the middle.

I asked Terence how I would introduce myself in the factory and he proceeded to give me a crash course in Mandarin. He suggested I say, 'Hello, I'm a designer and I've come to help you.' In Chinese, this is 'Nín hǎo, wǒ shì shè jì shī, wǒ men lái bang zhù nín' or, to go the whole hog, 您好，我是设计师，我们来帮助您.

Terence repeated this phrase to me over and over again, until I was convinced I had it down. I insisted on visiting the workers on my own, without any interpreter. I walked on to the factory floor, still mouthing the phrase I'd been taught, and came across a line of women, all sitting down at long benches, fettling (evening glaze on biscuit ware before firing). Who knows what they must have thought as I hove into sight. I straightened myself to my full height and duly recited my speech.

To this day I've no idea what I *actually* said to them, but it must have been hilarious, as they all fell about laughing, holding their hands over their mouths as they did so, which I noticed is what everyone did in China when they heard a good joke. Finally, one of the women calmed down enough to answer me.

'Yeah, you big guy,' she said. And then tapping her stomach, she added. 'You like Superman.'

They all start cracking up again. There was nothing I could do but grin and slowly walk away.

Being twice the size of most Chinese people, I got the impression that I was often viewed as a sort of benevolent Mr Blobby character. Once, at a restaurant, they made me sit on two chairs stacked on top of each other, as they thought a single one wouldn't take my weight. Sometimes people used to laugh merely seeing me, particularly women. I didn't mind; at least it got people on my side. It was often very humid and if I was working on the factory floor, as I insisted on doing sometimes, I'd take my shirt off, revealing my somewhat hairy torso. This would usually prompt some of the women to come over and take pictures of me with their phones. Then one of them would unashamedly let me in on my new nickname.

'You like big fat, white hairy gorilla,' they'd say, and everyone would fall about laughing again.

The Chinese did tend to be quite direct and literal in their translations, but I like to think it was all meant with a certain affection. I was glad I wasn't the type of person who was self-conscious, or easily offended. I wouldn't have lasted two minutes if I had been.

I felt very at home at the factory. It was situated in a peaceful semi-rural setting, in contrast to the frantic pace of life in a Chinese city like Chaozhou itself. It consisted of a series of high-ceilinged, open-plan barns constructed from bamboo, through which a welcoming cool breeze would blow. This would dissipate the often intense heat, and also the clouds of cigarette smoke.

I've never been a smoker and since it was banned from pubs and restaurants in Britain, you rarely smell it there now. Far fewer people seem to indulge in the disgusting habit. But the Chinese are the biggest smokers in the world by far, about 350 million of them, and that's a lot. It takes some getting used to it again, especially in the morning, when I would walk into the breakfast room wherever we were staying to be met by a great fog of exhaled tobacco. It didn't help that I would be missing out on my proper coffee, as they don't really do that, or dairy, in China, so it was a double whammy.

I can't say there were many other negatives. Of course, being China, there were still the protracted negotiations around money to be had. Thankfully, I could leave all that to Dom. The Chinese have a saying with regards to brokering a deal: no party is to lose face. This means there must be no humiliation or loss of respect. As a matter of fact, the term 'to lose face' originated among the British community in nineteenth-century China as a translation of the mandarin 'tu lien', which means being unable to show one's face in public due to disgrace.

In 1876, Sir Robert Hart, Britain's consular official to China, published *These From the Land of Sinim: Essays on the Chinese*

Question, which included this passage: 'The country [China] begins to feel that Government consented to arrangements by which China has lost face; the officials have long been conscious that they are becoming ridiculous in the eyes of the people.'

The phrase stuck and became associated with the Chinese concept of 'face' in business dealings. Dom did not have to spend too long thrashing it out. Ben Zhang and Yi Zhang had tried harder to impress us than any of the other factories we had visited and we were determined to secure their services. Dom offered to pay them above the price they had quoted us, a move that somewhat confused Ben Zhang, as this wasn't the way it was done in China. But we didn't care about losing face (or being called a big fat, hairy white gorilla). We just wanted them to make my pots.

We didn't take the decision to use the factory lightly. By the time we had made our minds up, Dom and I had visited on numerous occasions, to satisfy ourselves that all aspects of their business aligned with our own company values. By spending quality time with the staff and management, it was clear to us this was an extremely well-run operation. From my point of view, having spent a number of long days toiling among them on the shop floor, I could vouch for the industry and skill of the workforce, the majority of whom had worked there for years. Although they were paid well for their labours, this didn't seem to be a great motivating factor for them. Work was as integral to their lives as family was; something to be not endured, but embraced.

I'll never forget the first shipment of 28,000 mugs that we received at our warehouse back home. It would have taken me at least six months, working non-stop, to make that many. It was a big moment for me. It meant I was no longer tied to the wheel. The quality and consistency was incredible and beyond what I had ever thought possible. I was as proud of these mugs as I would have been of my own handmade ones.

I've come to love China and its people, especially its potters. The Chinese are not particularly quick at working, it's that they never stop. It gives me a buzz to go into the factory at one in the morning – as I have done once or twice – to see some people working away, oblivious of the time. It reminds me of the old Highgate Pottery days. They're workaholics. And they know a thing or two about making ceramics.

They are my kind of people.

16
POTS THAT TALK

Look carefully at this photograph. What do you think is going on here? Someone having a really bad day at Glastonbury, perhaps? The casual observer might not recognise this as art. But it is. In fact, it's a still from a piece of land art performance by the Dutch artist Alexandra Engelfriet. She is using her whole body to manipulate and reshape ten tons of wet clay that has been laid out in a trench twenty feet deep. I watched her do this in April

2016 at the Clay Gulgong festival in Australia and, if I sound flippant about it, that's because I was.

Beforehand, the prospect of having to watch it left me cold. Having worked so intimately with clay myself for over thirty years, you would think I'd have been more sympathetic, appreciating it as a valid extension of what I do myself most days sitting at my wheel, using my hands to create something new. But when I was introduced to Alexandra several days before her performance, I have to say I was armed to the teeth with prejudice.

For starters, I had never had much time for clay performance art – not that I had seen much of it, to be fair. To me, it was pure self-indulgence, gimmicky, lacking substance. Plus, Alexandra made me feel uncomfortable. I thought she seemed incredibly standoffish and arrogant. She was holding what I thought was a vape – though I never saw her take a puff from it – a mere affectation, I concluded. I rarely take against people so strongly; I'll usually give someone the benefit of the doubt, but my partner Marj and I both came away from the encounter thinking, she really needs to get over herself.

This seemed a minor blip in what was otherwise a mind-blowing event. Gulgong is a nineteenth-century gold rush town in the Central Tablelands district, 300 kilometres north-west of Sydney. The gold has long gone, but the town retains the sleepy characteristics of the past. When I arrived there, it reminded me of one of those Wild West towns that Clint Eastwood rides into at the start of a movie, before he kills everybody. But every two years Gulgong is transformed, as hordes converge for a full-on ceramic love-in. Leading artists mingle with pottery enthusiasts of every size, shape and nationality for a week-long series of workshops, lectures, private views and performances.

All the local shops, even the launderette, barber and estate agent, are used as galleries to display the work. Throw in the flawless weather and early morning presentations, where champagne and doughnuts are served, and you've pretty much got my idea of heaven.

The festival is run by the Mansfield family. It was started in 1989 by Janet Mansfield, a towering figure in Australian ceramics. She is revered for her wood firing; her work is represented in major public collections worldwide. She also wrote several major books on Australian and international ceramics and launched two internationally respected ceramics journals, *Ceramics: Art and Perception*, and *Ceramics Technical*. She is credited with elevating ceramics publications to a new level, combining her vast knowledge of the subject with an affinity for words and language.

Janet was initially attracted to Gulgong by its inexhaustible supply of exceptional white kaolin clay and she set up a studio there in 1977, where she continued to make her distinctive salt-glazed and anagama wood-fired vessels. Sadly, Janet died in 2013, but the festival is now in the capable hands of her daughter-in-law Bernadette, and son Neil. It was Bernadette who had invited me to the festival, quite out of the blue.

It was early in 2015. Australia couldn't have been further from my thoughts. I was sitting in my workshop on the north Kent coast, checking my emails one chilly morning. I get loads and loads of emails and I don't really do words, or reading. I prefer shapes, contours, and clean lines. Partly, this is down to my being dyslexic, but it's also a physical thing. It's much easier to ask someone for something rather than think about it and write it all down – for me, anyway. But, it has to be done.

So there I was, categorising the emails at speed: dreary, important, rude, annoying, scam, spam; I've won the Canadian lottery – again. Then I came to Bernadette's email. I had never heard of her or Gulgong, but she was offering to pay for me and an assistant to fly out to the next festival. I was gobsmacked – and it takes a lot to gobsmack me.

I thought there had to be a catch or a mistake, but subsequent emails and a delightful telephone conversation confirmed it as a genuine offer. What's more, Bernadette had selected me to be one of her festival Masters – an international panel of professionals working in the ceramics field, who speak and demonstrate their craft at the festival. I was hugely flattered, yet puzzled about how this stranger from across the globe had singled me out. I thought perhaps she had come across my Word Range, which we had recently started distributing down under. But no, it wasn't my pottery that had attracted her attention.

'I saw you dressed up as Adele, in *that* video.'

The Adele video!

Six feet four and sixteen stone of me, squeezed into a dress, stilettos and beehive wig, false eyelashes and more, singing my own warped version of 'Rolling in the Deep'. She meant *that* video. I should state, right now, that it was the brainchild of my business partner, Dom Speelman. The way he tells it, he was trawling YouTube one afternoon, seeking inspiration; his principal aim was to find different ways to humiliate me while emptying our warehouses of all their pots. He came across the Adele video, which is pretty odd in itself – at one point, a shadowy ninja figure is hurling crockery against the wall of a creepy-looking basement, for no apparent reason.

It was this image that got Dom thinking this could be the perfect vehicle for the next Make International promo. Well, he is a bit odd. What swung it for him were the viewing figures; 35

million, up to that point, making it one of the most viewed music videos of all time. Dom speed-dialled me and I heard his enthusiastic tones.

'Keith, have you ever heard of a singer called Adele?'

'Yes, Dom, I am currently living on Planet Earth, so I have indeed heard of her.'

Being in a different orbit, he didn't register the sarcasm. He told me how many views the video had totted up and I agreed it was the high side of a lot. I could tell Dom was excited and about to make an unusual request of me. I braced myself.

'The wife's auntie has a mansion not dissimilar to the one in the video. We could go up there and do our own spoof on Adele. You could dress up, you know, like her, and we could write new lyrics to the song, about pottery, about clay, and all that, and you could sing it.'

It came out just like that, in one breathless stream of logic-defying consciousness. The fact that I didn't hesitate to agree shows much about our relationship and Make International's screwball marketing strategy. No one could accuse us of being risk-averse.

A few weeks later, I was driving up to Suffolk for the shoot with my ten-year-old son by my side and the beehive in the boot. Brent Eleigh Hall is a substantial pile set in thirty-nine acres, but had seen better days. It was a fascinating place to explore while the film crew set up. Ned, my son, was stupidly excited at the prospect of being on a film set and was running in and out of the bedrooms, counting them all. Being ten, though, he soon got a bit bored, so I promised him he could help smash up the mugs in the mug-smashing scene. His eyes popped out of his head at the thought of that, but sadly, he soon realised that, like most things in life, filming was mainly boredom interspersed with hard work. He didn't even take much notice when his old man was squeezing himself into a dress and stilettos.

The video was really well put together and skilfully directed by Ness Whyte, who was a friend of Dom's wife, Phoebe. The finished piece *looked* fantastic. The combination of high production values, the bizarre kitsch-musical-horror vibe and my own lumbering presence hit some weird chord with the public and it quickly got a lot of exposure online. People, on the whole, were loving 'Rolling Clay with Keith'. Certainly Dom was a big fan, as our website was getting more hits and orders were on the rise. From my point of view, it was a difficult watch and listen. I looked like Widow Twankey after a bucket-load of steroids, and I thought my singing on it was simply awful.

The strongest reaction by far, though, was drawn from my wife at the time. She simply burst into tears when she saw it – and they weren't the sort of tears I routinely knock out at the sight of a half-decent pot. These were great bitter sobs. When she could speak, she told me I looked ridiculous and that I'd never be taken seriously as a potter ever again. I tried to point out the difference between being serious about your work and not being precious about what others think of you, but she wasn't having it; she was convinced I had committed career suicide.

She could not have been more wrong. Fast forward a couple of years and here I was, on the back of that video, being invited to the other side of the world to give lectures as a Master of my craft. And that wasn't all I had to thank 'Adele' for. That ridiculous wig and God-awful caterwauling had caught the attention of someone else, a person who would have an even greater influence over my future.

In the summer of 2014, Dom and I had been negotiating with an American businesswoman who owned a number of shopping malls over there. The deal never transpired, but this woman had a friend from England called Rich McKerrow, who was one of the creative directors at Love Productions.

At the time of our talks, he was over in the States pitching *The Great British Bake Off* series to various TV networks. He mentioned to her that he was looking for a new show format along the lines of *Bake Off*. In passing, she told him about the English nutters she had been speaking to, who had made this strange spoof video as a promotion for their ceramic range. Intrigued, Rich went back to his hotel room and watched the video. Boom! He phoned me and asked if I would be interested in making a programme with him about pottery.

I said I would. I was.

When we got back to Britain, Rich wanted to arrange an initial meeting to discuss the programme he had in mind. I was cagey. I certainly didn't think: Wow, I'm going to be on TV! I was anxious that developing the idea would take up a lot of my time, and then probably come to nothing. I was no big fan of *Bake Off* – to be honest, I had never really watched it, but I did think the format was an interesting way of demonstrating the ways people approach the creative process; I could definitely see it working with ceramics as well as it did with cakes.

In the end, being someone who has always tried to push the envelope and put myself out there, I knew I had to see how far 'Adele' could take me. One thought nagged away at me, though: was Rich expecting me to do the show in drag?

★   ★   ★

In the weeks leading up to the Gulgong trip, I was feeling increasingly anxious about the presentation I had been asked to give as one of the festival Masters. To be honest, I didn't feel like a master. I had bags of confidence in my ability as a potter, but the thought of standing up and being articulate in front of my peers terrified me. I had made my living and reputation by making affordable, functional pottery. I had never exhibited anything in my life, and my perception was that I was sure to be looked down upon by the ceramic artists, those who had studied at art school and regarded clay principally as a medium for fine art. I had a big chip on my shoulder about them not accepting me. On top of all this, I hadn't had a proper holiday in years and I plain needed a break.

It's a long journey to Australia, so we decided to break it up with stops in Hong Kong, China and Sydney, and by the time Marj and I arrived at the festival, we were both feeling more chilled out. The opening ceremony was held at the charming Prince of Wales Opera House, the oldest operating opera house in the southern hemisphere. There, I finally got to meet Bernadette Mansfield, who was a real lovey, but obviously determined that I should sing at the opening of the festival.

My anxiety started to bubble up at the thought. She was trying to persuade me to do the ceramic-themed cover of the Pharrell William's song 'Happy' – something I had done the previous summer for another promo. I threw out some excuses about not remembering the words, my larynx being 'fat' and not sufficiently limbered-up, and that besides, there was no way I could do it without backing. Cutting in, the house soundman irritatingly announced that he could get a backing track from the internet, no problem. What could I do? Everyone was so nice, I couldn't say no. Marj and I dashed back to the hotel so I could relearn the lyrics.

We sat outside our room with me playing, pausing, and rewinding the 'Happy' video on my laptop and Marj writing down the lyrics, neatly, so I could read them. Suddenly, a woman appeared, looking very concerned on our behalf. She pointed at something above our heads and shouted.

'What?' we replied.

In the end, we got the gist that if we didn't move, and quickly, we'd be pissed upon by a possum up in the tree above. It was only a matter of time, she added.

We gaped at each other, all dressed up, and scuttled off inside. Where it was very hot. And getting hotter. Mid-rewind, Dom called from England. He does pick his moments. He didn't want to wish me luck or anything, he wanted to know the ins and outs of the visit I had made to our factory in China on the way over. What with him bending my ear, trying to learn the words to 'Happy' and being stalked by an incontinent possum, I had no room left for nerves; the situation was so ridiculous, I just relaxed.

I reassured Dom everything was dandy and then we returned to the Prince of Wales, taking our seats as Bernadette was introducing Sharon Winsor, a Wiradjuri woman and one of the indigenous Australian aboriginals who are the custodians of the surrounding land. She sang a traditional song of welcome, a Wiradjuri song that acknowledged the earth beneath us and the coming together of different clans in a peaceable setting to celebrate and share knowledge. Visually striking, with white paint across her face and arms, Sharon had everyone enraptured. Although I was unable to understand a word, her song was deeply moving and a beautiful way to start the festival.

A little later on, I took the stage. My performance of 'Happy' didn't quite have the same mesmeric sense of occasion and drama, but the audience clapped along and an unexpected confetti explosion at the end brought it to a satisfyingly loud climax.

The next couple of days flew by. My first ever presentation went without a hitch. I even enjoyed myself. During the evenings I happily demonstrated my throwing, answered lots of questions and found myself in a tent singing 'Rolling Clay with Keith', unaccompanied.

The other Gulgong Masters were a joy to be around. We had travelled up from Sydney with two of them, Garth Clark and his partner Mark Del Vecchio, sharing a bumpy ride in a tiny chartered plane. We enjoyed a couple of late evenings with them in the pub next to our hotel, where I was humbled to learn that they knew of my work. For my part, I was ashamed that I had never heard of them. They were considered two of the leading authorities on modern ceramics, had won countless awards, written hundreds of books, essays and articles between them, and since 1981 had owned and run the Garth Clark Gallery in New York. For twenty-five years they had been a profound influence on the way ceramics was perceived as a valid art form in itself.

They were incredibly generous towards me, doing me the great honour of including my Word Range in the 'ceramic and design' section of their presentation. This was a real surprise, as they hadn't let on they were going to do it. It was intriguing to hear their take on the range: 'pots that talk', using words whose 'meanings changed depending upon how you read them'. To illustrate the point, they flashed up an image of one of my tea mugs with the word 'Love' stamped on it and reasoned this could either signify a 'command, a question, a suggestion or a cry of desperate loneliness.'

It was validation and thrilling for me to hear my work discussed from a conceptual point of view, in such an articulate and amusing way. Peculiarly, it was also a relief that someone had finally 'got me' and how I was expressing myself through my craft.

Ever since leaving school, I had shut myself away from this world, partly through being too busy to think further than the next day's workload, but more because of my own insecurities. I had spent most of my professional career in my studio making pots in order to eat, quite literally. I never had the time to organise an exhibition of my work and I suppose, in some ways, I resented missing out on that side of the world of ceramics.

From the early days of trying to establish my own business, I'd had a strong desire to explain fully why and how I do what I do and why it was so important to me, and now, at Gulgong, I had been given the opportunity to do precisely that. I felt proud to be considered a valued member of this worldwide creative community. All my preconceptions about not 'fitting in' were unfounded. Each of us excelled in a particular area of ceramics and there was a place for everyone. What really struck me was the lack of pretension and the knowledge, humility and sheer artistry of the other Masters. It may sound strange, considering my experience, but I can honestly say that being part of this event made me feel truly confident for the first time in my professional career. I felt I belonged.

It was halfway through this week I never wanted to end when I got a reality check and heard something that wiped the smug smile off my face in an instant. It concerned Alexandra Engelfriet, the artist whom I thought had looked down her nose at me. I learned that she was profoundly deaf and what I had thought was her 'vape' was a highly sensitive listening device connected to a receiver in her ear that helped her pick up sounds. The cool intensity, as I saw it, was in fact only her concentrating like mad on the lip movements of those around her, trying to follow the conversation.

I was mortified. I pride myself on being an open-minded person, and this was a sharp dig in the ribs, reminding me what an insensitive, judgemental plonker I am capable of being. I thought it showed me in a terrible light, especially when I considered how accepting everyone had been towards *me*.

Alexandra was due to perform her piece on the last day of the festival, and I have to say, I remained a bit sceptical about it. My attitude started to change as I approached the performance site. The Mansfields had dug an impressive trench and filled it with the wonderful local clay, a rich terracotta, full of iron from the soil and quite plastic in its consistency. Volunteers, mostly students from the Sydney School of Art, had been seconded for the week and stood on the edge of the trench dousing the clay with gallons of water in readiness for Alexandra to begin.

As I stood with hundreds of spectators on the bank opposite the trench, there was a palpable feeling that something special was about to happen. And it really did. The moment Alexandra got into the trench, a wave of emotion came over me that was totally unexpected.

It was mesmerising. So unusual; full of grace and vigour. I couldn't take my eyes off the slight but powerful figure, trance-like, totally as one with the clay, dancing with it and within it, forming new indentations, fissures and patterns with her arms, her legs, her torso, her whole being. I was so engrossed that I nearly toppled into the trench myself at one point.

It was such a fitting end to the festival, an artist literally melting back into the earth that gave up the clay in the first place. The performance made so much sense in the context of Alexandra's deafness; she seemed to compensate for the loss of her hearing by overloading her sense of touch.

I love the feel of wet clay in my hands, so I can only imagine the sensation when applied to the whole body. Watching her work was like a religious experience, one of the most moving and sensual things I have ever witnessed in my life. I could not believe I had ever doubted Alexandra Engelfriet. Her rolling in the mud and me sitting at my wheel. It is the same thing.

17
TV GOLD

By dawn on the first day of filming *The Great Pottery Throw Down*, I was a big bag of jangling nerves. Not because I was a judge: I know a lot about pottery, and I was comfortable with my ability in that department. But I knew very little, in fact virtually nothing, about making TV programmes, or being 'on the telly'. And here I was, about to start. I was really aware that a load of cameras were going to be pointing at me, *examining* me almost, and picking up on everything I said. I was desperate not to do or say the wrong thing.

At the start of the day, main presenter Sara Cox, my fellow judge Kate Malone and I were handed a call sheet, which is the running order for the day. On the bottom of the page it said in big red capital letters:

THE JUDGES' DECISIONS ARE FINAL. NO ONE IS TO INTERFERE WITH THE JUDGES' DECISIONS.

Reading that did the trick. Sort of. Instead of fretting over my own performance, I found myself starting to feel anxious on behalf of the potters. I thought of them waiting to find out what their first task would be. How must they be feeling? They had invested a great deal of themselves already to get to this stage. From hundreds of applicants, these ten talented people had been chosen to showcase their skills. I knew that on this first morning, there must be loads of nervous tension among them. After all, each had an equal chance of winning, but conversely, at the end of this first episode, one of them would be going home. And that decision would be down to Kate and me.

My responsibility for the task ahead was suddenly brought home to me. I felt an enormous amount of respect for all of the potters competing that day. It requires a great deal of courage to put yourself through a test like that. I wouldn't do it. I really wouldn't!

The very first task, or 'main make' as we were calling it, was to create a set of five nested bowls that would fit perfectly, each inside the other. It was very much a throwing challenge and had to be completed within a short timescale. As the session got underway, I was quickly able to gauge who was coping well and who was not. The minutes flew by, as if we were on fast-forward. I wanted everyone to do well, but found myself rooting for those who were struggling under the pressure.

It was evident that one of the potters, Rekha, was really up against it. I started shouting encouragement from across the room. I'm not sure that helped any, but I felt for her; it looked as if she was not going to finish her last bowl, the largest one – and that would probably mean that she'd be out of the competition.

'Rekha's in trouble! Get the cameras on her,' I heard the floor manager say to the director.

Of course, I'd been well aware that the jeopardy of the potters being up against the clock was where the drama would be. But I hadn't imagined it would be this tense, or that I'd feel so affected by it. Watching Rekha becoming more and more stressed made *me* feel stressed. I couldn't help but put myself in her shoes; this was the first task and it was looking as if she was going to fail to complete it. The tension was becoming unbearable. Something or somebody had to give. Unfortunately, it was me.

I started crying. I couldn't help it. It's something I have always done, I guess quite a lot, when I or friends or family are having a difficult time. But not generally when watching a stranger struggle with a piece of pottery! I tried to hold it in, but the tears came rolling down my cheeks. I felt embarrassed that I couldn't stop them.

Then I saw one of the camera-operators looking at me, open-mouthed, and heard the floor manager bellow: 'My God! One of the judges is crying … KBJ is crying!'

* * *

213

Okay, maybe I haven't always been a habitual open blubber. When I was young I was more a mimic of my father, who didn't like to show emotion, and therefore rarely did. So as a young man I wouldn't allow myself to cry in public, or in front of anyone for that matter. On the underneath, however, I was a sensitive person. I remember crying at Lucie Rie's exhibition at the V&A when I was seventeen; yes, one of her bowls was so beautiful it moved me to tears. Funnily enough, today I remember only my reaction, not the actual piece that moved me so much.

I think my emotions started to come to the surface as a result of my pottery work. 'Creating' became part of my daily working life and I gradually developed a deep empathy for other people who are creative, and their work. I know how much of oneself is invested in the process, whether that be talent, hard work or both. As I have grown older, however, I've found my tears flow more regularly when moved by anything or anybody, and it can still mortify me when it happens – mostly in front of friends. They have become used to it and generally laugh indulgently at me. I have also learned to live with it.

The year 2015, which was when we filmed that first series of the *Throw Down*, was an extremely emotional one for me, and it wasn't only art that brought on the waterworks. By then, my elderly father had been living in a care home for several years. He had never been good at looking after himself, but now things were worse and there was a clear reason behind it; he was suffering from dementia. That summer, as we began recording the *Throw Down*, he was fading before our eyes.

It's a strange experience, watching a parent become weaker than you. My mother's death had been sudden and totally unexpected, but with my father, you could see the sorry end from a very long way off. He underwent a slow decline that I truly

believe started on the day my mother died. In many respects, he gave up on life that day, or gave up caring, anyway. The family home in Walmington Fold quickly fell into disrepair, and so did my father. After a year or two, he sold the house for peanuts and rented a flat a few streets away.

I understood that he found it too painful to stay in the house and I thought it was a positive move, but I spent little 'quality time' with him from that point onwards. When I moved to Whitstable, he rarely visited and I don't believe he ever went up to see my sister Sarah at her home in Glasgow. He never showed any interest whatsoever in getting to know my son Ned, who was, after all, his only grandchild. It was odd behaviour and I have to say, I found it hurtful. I tried to bring it up with him, his lack of interest in his own family, but he would brush me off as he did whenever I tried to broach a difficult or personal subject. The door was always slammed shut on conversations like that.

I was aware from an early age that my father was a frustrated, angry man. As I got older, I learned that the root of the problem was a great 'what might have been'. I garnered this from only a few words uttered to me when I was about thirteen years old on one of those long, slow journeys around the North Circular, returning from watching London Welsh at Gunnersbury Park. This was when my father gave me the only piece of advice he would ever offer.

'Whatever you decide to do with your life,' he told me, 'don't do what I've done and do it just for the money. Make sure you do something you enjoy. Or your life will be miserable.'

That was it, more or less. He didn't add 'like mine' – he didn't need to. I understood that his life had been a disappointment to him. What compelled him to open his heart in that way, on that occasion, I've no idea. He never did it again. Perhaps that's why I took notice. I never forgot his words.

What my father loved above all else was sport. He was good at it, and it's probable he would have been able to make a living out of it, if the choice had been down to him. He was a very good tennis player, but football was the game at which he really excelled, and in his teens he was offered an apprenticeship with West Ham United.

In those days, though, during the mid-1950s, footballers did not enjoy the mammoth wages of today's top-flight players. If he'd been good enough to play for the first team, he would have been paid around £15 per week, which was decent money – double the average working wage of the time. However, a footballer's career was over by the time he was in his thirties and the pragmatic view, held by my parental grandfather, was that my father would struggle to find another career at that age.

Knowing my father's nose-thumbing attitude towards authority in his later life, I do wonder why he paid heed to his father and dutifully went into shipping insurance. But I also know that 'Pa' was a very forceful character, so maybe at the time that fateful decision was made, my father simply lacked the strength and certainty to go against him. Whatever the reason, that career choice changed the course of his life and, as he put it, 'made him miserable'.

Besides sport, the only other period of his life I remember him discussing with enthusiasm was his National Service days, which he spent serving with the army in Holland. Despite smashing his face into an iron girder when larking about (his nose was totally wonky thereafter), he really enjoyed his time there. He walked into his regiment's football team, of course, which was doubly excellent for him, because it meant he got extra food rations. I also remember his stories about the nightlife there being much more fun and relaxed than in England. He used to talk about the transvestites in the bars openly dancing with the soldiers, about how it was tolerated, and I think this appealed to his broadminded outlook on life.

He once compared those Dutch nights out to the experience of going to see the Wigs live. He said the atmosphere of the venues we played reminded him of his National Service days. That was one of the few conversations I ever had with him about my being in a band, and yet he came to most of our gigs, would you believe?

Often, he wouldn't even say hello to me. I think he was mindful of allowing me my own space, or maybe he thought I wouldn't want to be seen talking to my father, I don't know, but I thought it was great that he came to see us. There would be all these young indie kids, punks and psychobillies, with their mad hairdos and leather and make-up, and then there would be my father in his anorak, standing at the back, totally at ease with it all. He would always come on his own, but he'd generally start up a conversation with someone or other.

He had been very fit in middle age, but the strain on his body of years of playing football and tennis took its toll, and eventually he had to have both hips replaced. He was never the same after that, as he never regained his previous agility and mobility. His physicality had gone. That's when he began to display signs of dementia. It seemed as if he couldn't function at all if he couldn't play sport, and his body and mind simply began the process of shutting down.

By the end of April 2015, when I was due to start filming in Stoke-on-Trent, his decline had progressed to the stage where he didn't seem to recognise even food anymore. Sarah and I were expecting the worst.

★   ★   ★

In a way, it was a relief to begin work on the *Throw Down*. From my first meetings with Rich McKerrow of Love Productions the previous year, the whole process of acquiring the role of judge had been drawn out and stressful. I'd had to go through a series of screen tests, five of them over a period of six months to be precise, all up against other prospective judges. I was very aware that I might end up not being chosen at all, and I found this uncertainty difficult. On top of this, I was busy with my proper job and trying to fit in a screen test in east London is tricky when you're flying back and forth to China.

I finally heard I'd got the green light during a Make International team meeting in Whitstable, so we were all able to celebrate together. However, I was still to be convinced that a programme featuring pottery could be a winner. I believe I may even have remarked on this to Rich McKerrow, saying that the process might be like watching paint dry.

I knew it couldn't be the same as *The Great British Bake Off*. You can bake a cake in two hours; ceramics that require two firings can take up to 24 hours, and then they might need three days to dry out. How would that work on screen? Rich reassured me that they had taken all that into account; the *Throw Down* would fully embrace the art and skill of pottery and his editors would take care of the time lapses.

'Honestly, Keith,' he told me, 'I don't want to make car crash TV!' I had to laugh.

There would be no contestants appearing in the programme, as instead they would be referred to throughout as potters – a very positive point, I thought, which showed due respect to those taking part. Rich spoke with such passion about his vision for the *Throw Down* that eventually I stopped worrying and started looking forward to it. I felt I was in excellent hands.

It was an inspired decision to secure Sara Cox as the presenter of the show. Kate Malone and I had no experience of making programmes for TV, so to have someone as professional and laid-back as Sara to keep us in check was very reassuring. Like all pros, she makes something that is really not easy look like a doddle. And we all got on famously from the start – even though Sara got my name wrong three times.

That summer I covered a great many miles on the motorways. I was constantly up and down between Whitstable and Stoke, stopping off regularly in London to the Make International office, or to visit my father at his care home. The staff there were wonderful, and despite him being a cantankerous old sod, they liked him. Visits to see him were depressing at the time, but now looking back seem quite comical.

Marj and I would sit with my father in a room full of people (other residents), whom he would then proceed to slag off. Every time. One by one. 'See him …,' he would start, and point his finger. Luckily, but also quite sadly, none of his targets were ever alert enough to notice they had drawn his ire. He still recognised me and knew my name, but when I tried to tell him what was going on in our lives, or if I mentioned how Ned was doing at school, his face would be totally blank. If there was sport on TV when we visited, we'd be lucky to get even a blank look between us, because his eyes would be superglued to the screen. In many ways, nothing had changed from my childhood days; sport came first.

By the time we had got to filming episode four, I was pretty exhausted, emotionally. By now my father was bed-ridden and had to be fed by a carer, although he ate very little. He was wasting away. I had to inform the producers of the *Throw Down* that he might die at any moment. I was acutely aware that my having to leave suddenly, should this happen, would be very costly to the whole production. The whole team had been very supportive of me, in fact we'd become like an extended family. When I came in around 6 a.m. each day, everyone would greet me and ask how my father was doing.

On the morning of 28 May, I ambled in and was greeted by one of the executive producers, who asked the usual question. He stopped in his tracks when I told him my father had passed away in the night. I could see the blood drain out of his face. I have a feeling he was simultaneously processing how he would have to shut down production and put everyone on standby, while also trying to be totally sympathetic to my loss. I put my hand on his shoulder.

'Don't worry, though,' I reassured him. 'I've had a word with my sister and we're going to put him on ice until we've finished the episode.'

His mouth dropped open. He didn't know whether to laugh or cry, or both.

'Oh, thank you, really, that's great news,' he said after collecting himself.

I had to laugh at the situation. My father would have laughed too, if he'd been there. If nothing else, I'd inherited his sense of humour.

My father's funeral was days after my fiftieth birthday, in a scheduled filming break. There was a good turnout for him. Of course, some old London Welsh players came along and said nice things about him – in many ways, they were as much family to him as Sarah and I were. I didn't grieve for him afterwards, as I'd already done that when his dementia was diagnosed and the man I knew withdrew into himself. I think he was a tormented soul, my father, but at least now he was at peace. We scattered his ashes in Kent.

* * *

Once all the episodes were in the can and we'd said our final goodbyes to my father, I was desperate to get back to a bit of 'normal': design work, Make International, visits to Chinese factories, walks on the beach, maybe catching up with old friends. God knows, I had some catching up to do.

As luck would have it that August, for the first time in twenty-five years, the old Wigs band members were planning on getting together for a bit of a reunion. I couldn't wait. We would meet down in Devon, at the sprawling home of Chris, who'd been our manager all those years before, and who had sold a London two-up two-down and bought a whole former art school. It promised to be a strange and wonderful couple of days. It was also very handy, because the *Throw Down*'s producers had asked if they could use a clip of a Wigs' video as part of a montage in the opening episode, to give viewers a glimpse into my background. I had to clear this with the other band members, of course, and get their signatures. Now I had the perfect opportunity to do so – in person!

We had kept in touch over the years, of course, but us all being together was a very rare occurrence – mostly because Mungo, our lead guitarist extraordinaire, had emigrated to New Zealand back in the noughties. Yes, he'd moved as far away from the rest of us as he possibly could. But that August he was coming back for a special holiday, courtesy of beautiful bassist and amazing musical all-rounder Stuart, who had paid for his trip out of a recent inheritance.

As is generally the case when you meet up again with old friends, we quickly picked up from where we'd left off and laughed, partied, sang and pranced about like we were all twenty-one again. We'd all had our problems and hardships to overcome, but it seemed like everyone was getting there, and doing all right.

Stuart had been the only one of us to develop any proper sort of career in music. He was making a decent living singing in a pub covers band – but not any sort of pub covers band, this one played regular spots at all the best central London pubs and had made a real name for themselves. Stuart was lead singer, which was odd, because during his time with the Wigs he'd only ever sung backing vocals; we had been unaware he had this amazing voice. But that was Stuart all over; he was a real dark horse.

When we went to the beach on that first day, Stuart came along in the car with me and Marj, so we had the opportunity for a good chat. The last few times we'd met, he had always been in a new relationship with a younger, blonde woman; the relationships never lasted. This time, he was firmly single and seemed to be much more philosophical about life. He'd given up smoking and taken up yoga.

He told us an anecdote about his last girlfriend and how he'd woken up one morning and walked into the kitchen to find her parents sitting there. As they had chatted, he had slowly realised that even *they* were much younger than him, and that they had few shared reference points. It was like his situation with their daughter. It made us laugh when he recounted it, but it was also incredibly sad in a way, and Stuart knew that. On the same journey he confided that he'd suffered from depression for many years and had been on medication for it. I was so surprised. I'd had no idea about this. I had seen Stuart as such a classic happy-go-lucky, rock 'n' roll kind of bloke. He was always smiling. And he smiled all that little holiday in Devon.

Two weeks later, on August bank holiday Monday, I got a call from Mick. I knew immediately from the break in his voice that something was very wrong, but I could not have imagined how wrong. He told me that Stuart had taken his own life the night before. He'd cut his wrists. I broke down, and then I felt numb. In all the years I had known Stuart, I hadn't really known him at all. Only now did I understand him better, and it was too late. He was gone. And he'd gone all alone.

Over the next few hours, I thought about what he had told us in the car on the way to the beach and it took on a whole new significance. We still muse, now, about whether he was deliberately saying goodbye to us all during that short trip to Devon, and whether that had been behind his decision to fly Mungo over from New Zealand. We will never know for sure.

Stuart was a wonderfully talented and much-loved man, who was a treasured part of so many lives. Many, many people attended his funeral to underline those facts, to remember him and to show each other how loved Stuart had been. Only Stuart, for some reason, could not see it, or if he did, it was not enough for him.

I truly miss him. We all do.

*   *   *

The Great Pottery Throw Down was aired on BBC2 in November and December 2015 to very good reviews. It was hard watching myself on TV to begin with, but I guess I got used to it. We'd invite friends over for a glass of wine and a cheese board and watch it on the big screen, cheering, jeering and laughing – mostly at me. The programme really did raise pottery's profile and inspired more people to give it a go, which was a big positive for me.

There was, predictably, a bit of a hoo-hah about my tears. Some people found them an uncomfortable watch, while others thought emotion from a man was refreshing. For my own part, it was frustrating not being able to control it. It is difficult trying to get words out when you start to blub, as you end up making this horrible, high-pitched squeak. I remember, during filming of the last episode, I was standing there with Sara and Kate on either side of me.

'I really hope I don't cry judging the final,' I confided in them. 'It's getting on my nerves. I can't get my words out properly.'

The director must have heard, because she came running out to me.

'Whatever you do, KBJ,' she said, 'Don't stop crying! It's TV gold.'

I don't know about that, but it did help to create a buzz around the programme. Suddenly, I was getting recognised in public. I remember flying off to China following that first series and I did about thirty selfies with people between the gate and boarding the plane. It was mad!

My favourite story about being spotted in public happened when I was on a shopping trip with Ned in London. He doesn't watch TV and, to this day, has never watched an episode of the *Throw Down*. I believe he thinks I exaggerate about how popular it is, and how good it is. Anyway, we were walking through Soho when two teenage girls approached us. To me, they didn't look like the types who would watch a programme about pottery, but as they drew level with us, one of them gasped, turned to the other and said: 'It's Potman!' Then they both giggled.

Hmmm, Potman. I'll take it over Mr Blubby, I suppose.

18

AN EARLY
CHRISTMAS PRESENT

There was a time – not that long ago in months and years, but another lifetime away in terms of Covid, lockdowns and all the rest – that my life was getting so busy, sometimes I didn't know where I was. I would muse over the ins and outs, the expense, the lack of sleep and my carbon footprint, but business travel was important; often, I had to go physically to a facility to check things out to my satisfaction. Video calls can't do everything for you.

I was spinning those metaphorical plates as fast as I could, covering miles to keep everything up in the air, dashing around … It was fun, but also crazy – and a complete turnaround from the first twenty years of my career, when the furthest my work took me was Oxford, only fifty miles from London. I'd drive out there on the M40 to deliver pots to Habitat's warehouse. The only other time I'd desert the potter's wheel would be for a trade fair, and in those days I visited only the London-based ones.

Now here I was in 2018, coming into land at Indira Gandhi International Airport in New Delhi, the Indian capital city. I would be staying for two days only and I would not be seeing any of the sights. Not for me the Taj Mahal or the Red Fort; I was here for one thing only. I'm sure you can guess what that was. Yes, I was visiting a ceramics factory. Twenty-four hours earlier I'd been on the set of *The Great Pottery Throw Down* at Middleport, watching the remaining four contestants hand-build their intricately designed, themed toilets. That week was full of contrasts, and summed up perfectly the bonkers scheduling challenges my life at that time would throw up.

It was semi-final week, so there was quite a buzz around the set. The potters had worked so hard to get to this point and none of them wanted to be the one to miss out on the final. It was a difficult, if surreal challenge, with four separate parts that needed designing and fitting together: the pedestal, the bowl, the rim and the U-bend. That was a lot of clay – in fact it would turn out to total the largest amount we had used in a single episode up until that point.

We were using tandoor clay, one of the strongest available in ceramics. They build cylindrical ovens with it – yes, the ovens where tandoori chicken is cooked – and they're used for cooking all over Asia. The clay was rough and felt like wet cement. I don't think the contestants had much experience of using it – I hadn't.

I envisaged some cracking problems could emerge after the drying and firing. We'd had regular occurrences of potters' work cracking on the programme. It is one of the occupational hazards of being a potter, although it can be largely avoided if great care is taken. There are many reasons why pottery cracks. To avoid it, you need consistency: in thickness, in the amount of glaze applied, and in the time taken to dry for each piece. The problem is, when you're up against the clock and stressing about whether you are going to finish on time, a consistent approach is probably the last thing on your mind. I don't know how the contestants cope with that aspect. My need to have things 'just so' makes it very difficult for me.

Take this toilet challenge, for example. The build required a number of structural joins where the thickness of the clay would naturally vary. Then there would be the added decorative touches and even more thick layers. One of the contestants, Ryan, had decided to build a turtle toilet, with its head poking out the front and the shell being the lid. It was a bold and original design, but I was concerned he might be trying to do too much, particularly with the amount of clay being used.

There is a lot of water in clay before it dries, about 20 per cent. As it dries it shrinks – some clay does so more than others – which is another problem to contend with if you're not familiar with it. Parts of the clay build that are thinner will naturally dry quicker than the thicker parts. This in turn puts the pottery under strain, which can cause cracking and large amounts of on-set angst. I guess it all adds to the drama of the episode.

The second day of filming the toilet challenge was a Sunday. Being the semi-final, things were even more tense than usual and like everyone else on set, I was being drawn further into each contestant's quest to impress us. It was no surprise to me when cracks appeared as the toilets were drying out, but thankfully none of these were serious. We took a break and, as I can't help doing, I checked my emails. Right away, I spotted the one from my office I'd been half-expecting. It confirmed that I was to fly off to India the next morning!

The urgency was real. We were hoping to launch a new Make International range by Christmas, which would be a collaboration with Hokolo, a company based in London and headed up by Jen Taylor, who hailed from my new stomping ground of Hong Kong. Her striking, geometric patterns perfectly complemented a 1970s-inspired stackable ceramic collection I'd designed. I wanted everything to be made in bone china and had earmarked a factory in India to make them for us, but what with the filming and everything else, I hadn't found the time yet to get over to see them.

As it was now mid-July, we were up against it if we wanted to get the range out in time for the festive season. Then Love Productions sent me an early Christmas present: the toilet challenge! After the initial two days of hand-building, they had scheduled in a five-day filming break to allow time for everything to dry out. This was just enough time for my trip to India.

It might sound a bit over the top, swanning off to the subcontinent, but I had to go. I had to see for myself the quality of the factory's work, the conditions there, and the relationship between the staff and the management. It would be my name on the finished product, after all. Besides, the factory, Arta Broch Ceramics, was already working on another project of ours and I wanted to check how that was progressing as well.

I'd met the owners, Rishabh and Neel Patel, at the Ambiente Trade Fair in Frankfurt. The pair of them had permanent cheerful smiles on their faces, which was quite infectious. It was clear they loved what they did and that they were genuinely proud and excited about their business. After visiting their stand, I understood why: the bone china they had on display was some of the finest I'd ever seen. In fact, it was so good it made me quite emotional, and I had a good cry. The two brothers were quite amused to see me blubbing at the sight of their ceramics. In fact, I think it may have helped to clinch the deal!

And so, I was up at the crack of dawn on the Monday morning to begin my long journey out to see the guys at their factory at Vadodara, a city 1,000 kilometres south-east of New Delhi. It felt strange to be going all the way to India to visit, of all things, a bone china factory. You see, despite its name, this ceramic is a completely British invention. In this country during the eighteenth century, potters strove to recreate the hard-paste porcelain (also known as true-porcelain) used in China and East Asia, but they simply couldn't manage it. Instead, they developed a soft-paste version, adding animal bones to give it strength.

The formula for what was then called Staffordshire bone-porcelain was perfected by Josiah Spode in 1797. His was excellent timing. With import duties on Chinese porcelain becoming exorbitant – rising to 108 per cent in 1799 – the market was ripe for the taking, and subsequently all the major companies such as Minton, Derby and Worcester joined Spode in producing and selling fine bone china in vast quantities. Its popularity was further boosted in 1806 by the patronage of King George IV. He had become an avid collector and after inspecting the Spode factory, he showed his appreciation by making Josiah Spode 'Potter to His Royal Highness the Prince of Wales'.

For the next 200 years, bone china was made exclusively in England, at Stoke-on-Trent to be precise. It is still made there, but predictably, China is the now the world's largest manufacturer of it, and other producers like India, Russia and Iran are not far behind.

*　　*　　*

I landed in New Delhi after dark. It was disorientating to arrive in a strange country and then be driven straight to a hotel that, frankly, could have been in any city in the world. At least on the way, though struggling to keep my eyes open, I got a glimpse of life on the streets of the Indian capital.

It was teeming with life. Every shop was still open though the evening was wearing on. The roads, like the pavements, were jam-packed, but somehow everything was moving. Vying for space with my taxi were vehicles of every kind: buzzing mopeds cut across us as if we didn't exist; great prehistoric lorries honked their horns; cyclists were weaving in and out on suicide missions; and within inches of all this, sitting by the side of the road, families cooked their evening meals. I wanted to see more of all this, but sadly that wasn't possible. I was here for business, not pleasure.

The next day, I was up bright and early once again for the ninety-minute flight to Vadodara. It's a small city by Indian standards with a population of three and a half million. Beyond that I can't say much as Rishabh and Neel picked me up from the airport and took me directly to the factory, where we spent the entire day going through the finer points of the order we'd placed with them. By the end, I had no quibbles whatsoever with their facility or their capabilities. The work they'd already produced for us was first-class and I knew they would make a good job of the new Hokolo stackable range.

Although they'd been in business for three years, the factory looked brand-new and almost spotless. All the staff were friendly and polite, speaking to me in very good, though somewhat old-fashioned English, like actors in a 1950s black-and-white film. I always feel ashamed that I can't speak any of the languages of the places I visit. The British are lucky that others learn our language and, generally speaking, don't give us a hard time for not doing the same with theirs.

Being in the factory all day, I kind of forgot where I was, so it was a bit of a shock to go back outside and find India there before me with all its unique sights and smells. Rishabh and Neel kindly invited me to dinner at one of their apartments. They were great company and we ate the most exquisite meal cooked by one of their chefs. The brothers had obviously done very well for themselves, I thought, as I looked out from their balcony at the city of Vadodara.

The next morning my whistle-stop tour was over. I took a flight back to New Delhi and then waited for my connection back to Heathrow. Air travel is lost time for me. The next thing I knew, it was Thursday and I was sitting in the studio in Whitstable. India felt a bit like a dream, albeit a pleasant one. I caught up with Make International business, went through my emails, had lunch with Marj, and went for a swim to try to shake off the dream-feeling.

By Saturday lunchtime, I was back in Middleport to read the notes for the second phase of the toilet episode, which would focus on decorating the toilets, firing them, and then announcing the potter of the week and who would be leaving. That last bit is never an easy job – and it gets harder towards the end of a series, when you've got to know the potters better.

Long before I became involved with the *Throw Down*, I'd been racking my brains to think of ways I could promote the craft and ceramics industry. I wanted to give something back to it, but that proved difficult for an unknown potter. I guess that was one of the reasons behind the promotional videos that Dom and I made, dressing up as Adele and crooning my way through 'Happy': they were very unsubtle ways to get us and our pottery noticed.

I suppose deep down, I have a need to perform. I didn't necessarily miss it in those years after the Wigs split up, but having spent most of that time solely preoccupied with my business, I think it became very positive for me to have another outlet again, or another string to my bow, if you like. It can be a hard watch seeing yourself up on the screen, especially the close-ups, but I have to go through it. It helps me figure out how I'm coming across.

I've always been self-critical of anything I do; it keeps you on your toes and helps you improve in whatever you're trying to achieve. Before the first series, I had some training with TV presenter coach Ian Blandford. He gave me tips and advice on how to be natural in front of the cameras, which is not that easy. He told me one thing that made the penny drop with regards to how I should approach the task ahead: I had to try to convince the bloke in the pub that I was genuine – not try to be clever or play up to the camera, but to act as I would in everyday life. And that's what I try to do. Although I am performing, in a sense, when I'm in front of the camera, I am trying my hardest just to be me.

The success of the *Throw Down* was a tribute to the whole Love Productions team. Behind the scenes there is so much work required before and after the cameras are rolling, let alone before the series goes to air. It amazes me how the editors take days' worth of footage and make up a coherent episode. It's a real art condensing what is a long, drawn-out process into a flowing and compelling narrative.

The real stars, though, are the potters. During every series I've been inspired by their creativity and spirit, their ability to overcome fears and doubts and to push themselves beyond what they had believed themselves capable of doing. What I really love about them all – and this is what chokes me up – is their deep love of pottery. That absolutely comes across on the screen and I think that's the key element that keeps viewers tuned in.

There is no doubt that the programme has raised the profile of pottery in Britain and inspired more people to give it a try. After the first series, the craft supplier Hobbycraft reported a sizable increase in sales of all pottery-related products, and studios across the country were getting more people booking to do evening courses in ceramics.

I have noticed a definite shift in attitudes, too. For years, especially those when I was still hand-making everything, I would regularly get people visiting my studio or my stand at a trade fair who would pick up a mug and forthrightly tell me: 'I'm not paying twenty pounds for a mug!' Their whole manner suggested they thought I was ripping them off. This would even occur later on, with the lower-priced, factory-made mugs. It really used to get me – it wasn't like I was raking it in. I dare say the same people wouldn't baulk at paying the same price for a couple of gin and tonics in a bar, or for two coffees and cake at some motorway service station.

I'm glad to say this happens only rarely these days. There is far more appreciation of the craft and sweat that goes into making something and most people happily pay the price. I'm certain this is all linked to people developing an interest in pottery through watching the *Throw Down*; I hope it is, anyway, as it further validates why we are doing it.

By the time we reconvened at Middleport on the Sunday, a week had passed. The toilets had all dried out and been biscuit fired. There were a few small cracks, but nothing that would cause huge problems. Talking of cracks, they were starting to show on me, as I was now cultivating a painful stye in the corner of my eye, which is something of a facial disaster when you are about to go in front of a camera. I wanted to look my best when I was sitting on the toilets.

Oh yes, I forgot to mention, part of the judging criteria for the toilets was how comfortable they were to sit on. It would have been ungentlemanly of me to allow my fellow judge, Kate Malone, to do the honours in that respect. I only hoped the potters had taken into account my bulk when they were designing their pedestals.

The last day of filming an episode is always the most emotionally charged. It's when the potters retrieve their main make from the kiln. Even I feel a rise of panic when that door is opened. I know only too well that feeling you get when a firing is over and you're wondering if you're going to find pots or pieces inside.

This time it was all smiles from the potters as everything was brought out intact. Visually, all the finished toilets looked amazing; each one was totally unique to the potter who created it – I love that aspect of the programme, the fact that everyone had the same brief, but you got such varied results. To my great relief, the pedestals were good and sturdy and stood up to me sitting down on them. I'd never have lived it down if one had collapsed underneath me.

They all flushed, too, although some more forcefully than others. In terms of decoration, I was moved by Richard's Victorian meadow theme, especially the exquisite butterflies featured, and they caused my own waterworks to kick in, briefly. However, taking everything into account, Kate and I were unanimous that Ryan's Tina the Turtle should win Ryan the 'Potter of the Week' title for the semi-final. I was delighted he'd proved me wrong and pulled off a bold and imaginative build. He was fully aware that he had been taking a risk but went for it regardless. Sometimes that is the difference between winning and losing; you have to take a chance and not play safe. It's a good attitude to have in life.

By the way, we managed to get our Hokolo stackable range out in time for Christmas. I have some of them on the shelf in my workshop and can't look at them now without thinking back to that crazy week when I travelled 8,000 miles to spend a day in a city called Vadodara and then came back to be filmed sitting on a toilet with a turtle's head poking out between my legs.

It will take some beating, that.

19

ABSENT TRIBES

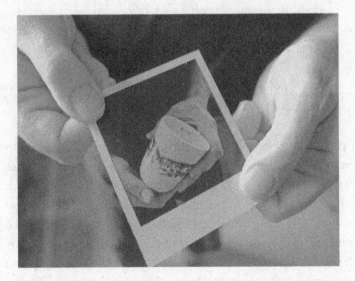

In the Romance of Commerce none is more worthy to find a place than Josiah Spode, his son, and grandson, who with assurance, art, and enthusiasm founded and maintained the Ceramic Factory in Staffordshire from which so much that is beautiful and fine emanated.

– T.G. Cannon, *Old Spode*, published
by T. Werner Laurie Ltd, London, 1924

Former employees of the
Spode Factory, Stoke-on-Trent:

- *It was 1948 when I started here; straight from school, with a load of friends from the same school. So we were all happy here straight away. We got one pound, fourteen and threepence a week.*
- *When you'd done twelve months, you went on a different system altogether and it was called 'earning by the dozen'. The 'dozen' altered compared to what ware you got. Like, saucers were eighteen in a dozen. There were fifteen cups in a dozen. Ten-inch plates were nine in a dozen, which was quite bad work, because you've got a lot more to paint on. So you tried to avoid ten-inch plates.*
- *It was a friendly, family atmosphere. Mother, father, daughter, grandmother, aunties, uncles; whole families really.*

I've had the honour, a few times recently, of being asked to create something original for an exhibition. It is liberating to explore and utilise other mediums and even to collaborate with other artists – a rare opportunity for me to branch out beyond making ceramics that are purely functional. So I was thrilled when Darren Washington, head of the Centre Space Gallery at the Spode factory site, asked me to contribute to an exhibition to coincide with the 2019 British Ceramics Biennial in Stoke-on-Trent that autumn. The brief was to create an installation that celebrated its workforce.

The Spode story encapsulates that of the British Potteries. A ceramic giant throughout the eighteenth and nineteenth centuries, it was at the cutting edge of new technology. That is, until its sad decline during the second half of the twentieth century. The Spode factory finally closed in 2008 after over 230 years of continual production. We called the exhibition 'Echoes of Spode

– Absent Tribes' to highlight the fact that although the buildings still stand, the people who spent their lives working there remain in spirit only.

The project was to be a real team effort. Alongside myself and Marj, who was art coordinator, we were joined by former Spode artistic director, Paul Rogerson; photographer, Sarah Peart; and installation facilitator, Dan Thompson. We decided that Spode employees would be the main focus, but we also wanted to reflect and celebrate the wider communities that were created around all the city's ceramic factories back in its heyday.

Around the beginning of the twentieth century, Spode's factory employed 1,100 men, women and children. My aim for this project therefore was to hand-make a porcelain beaker for each one of those workers: 900 large ones to represent the adults, and 200 smaller ones for the children – mainly 'clay boys', who balled up and prepared the clay.

When it came to the design of the beakers, it was a no-brainer: they would have to be adorned with the classic Spode 'Italian Blue' decoration. Josiah Spode, who founded the factory in 1770, was a great innovator. One of his greatest achievements was perfecting the process of underglaze blue transfer printing onto earthenware. This method of decorating pottery had been around in Britain for some time in various forms, but Spode's intervention allowed the process to be repeated on a large scale. Ingenious in conception, it involved engraving the design onto a copper plate, with holes of different size, shape and depth being meticulously cut into it by a master engraver.

It was highly skilled work and very labour intensive, taking about two months to complete a dinner plate design. Once the design was finished, a cobalt colour was heated and applied to the copper plate and a thin pottery tissue applied, allowing the colour to soak in. The tissue was then removed, cut to the size of the ware and applied to unglazed pottery. To complete the transfer, the tissue would be rubbed vigorously onto the ware, which was then washed to remove excess colour, glazed and fired.

Spode used this technique to produce the first printed willow-patterned pottery, which became extremely popular in England and made Spode a wealthy man. As I mentioned earlier, Spode was also responsible for perfecting the recipe for bone china, the English version of Chinese porcelain, renowned for its strength and resistance to chipping.

Unfortunately, he died before he could see the true fruition of his two great advancements, but they were fully utilised by his son, also called Josiah. The son did not inherit his father's flair for ceramics, but he was, perhaps, Britain's first great marketing genius, with a knack for spotting a fashion and exploiting it.

Now, in the early nineteenth century, the well-heeled English gentleman had two things on his wish list: to travel to Italy and to collect Japanese Imari porcelain – although not necessarily at the same time. Spode Junior had a hunch that if he integrated these two highly a-la-mode elements into a porcelain product, he might have something big on his hands. He was right; the Spode Blue Italian range of porcelain was a huge and immediate success, becoming a true British design classic.

So it had to be Blue Italian for my tribute Spode beakers. I didn't have to use the traditional method of getting a copper plate engraved and applying the blue transfer. Today, thankfully, I could simply take photographs of historical Spode designs and redraw them digitally, taking hours not weeks. I was so pleased with the results: my 1,100 beakers looked great, even if I do say so myself.

The plan was that the beakers would be arranged en masse, floor to ceiling in places, dominating the constricted gallery's visual space, while the workers' voices themselves would be heard in a shifting soundscape that moved from one set of reminiscences to the next as visitors moved around the installation. The exhibition was completed by factual textboards giving more of the place's history, along with wonderful photographs of the employees back-in-the-day and now, and historic views of the factory, its advertisements and its wares.

It was a wonderful project to be a part of. Together with the Biennial, it generated a good deal of great publicity for the old factory, attracting new visitors and providing a real boost to the ongoing regeneration of the site. For me, the most interesting and moving aspect was meeting the old employees who came along to visit the exhibition and see what we'd done. Their testimonies were the backbone of the whole show and it was fascinating listening to these elderly men and women, full of character and life, talking so fondly about the factory. It was clear how important their jobs had been to them.

In fact, it was clear they had not simply been 'jobs', and Spode had not just been a workplace; their work and the factory itself had been at the very heart of their lives. Witnessing how moved they were to be back at the factory was more than worth the effort of making all those beakers.

*　　*　　*

- *A boy came from the clay end, carrying a piece of clay. He kept coming past, every day.*
  'Hello, Pauline,' he said. 'Are you going to the dance?'
  I said, 'Yes. My mother said I can go.'
  He said, 'Could I take you?'

So I said – I hadn't a boyfriend then – I said, 'Ooh yes, I'll go with you.'

And he hired a dress suit to go with and he met me at the door, and these girls who were in the bob shop said, you know: 'Pauline, you're going to have the sack. You aren't supposed to be going out with somebody from the Clay end. We're china paintresses.'

So I had to tell him I couldn't go out with him. I must have broken his heart.

- *Christmas was great, snogging all the bosses; snog everybody in sight.*
- *I can't tell you how kind people were there. There was a girl who got herself in trouble. In them days you had no help and so we had a tin on my desk and we got enough money to buy her a cot and a pram.*

Typically, when the glory days of Stoke-on-Trent are celebrated, it is the men who get most of the credit, and pretty often those men are called Josiah: Wedgwood, Spode the First and Spode the Second. Right from the start, the best jobs were reserved for men, and only boys could be apprenticed to learn the trade, so in the early years of the industry, women were used as nothing more than labourers for their husbands and fathers.

Following the industrial revolution, as more factories were built and a larger workforce was required, more women were taken on to work at semi-skilled repetitive tasks, such as slip-casting and transfer printing. Like so many factory jobs in those days, life and labour was cheap and it could be a dangerous occupation. Girls as young as nine toiled in terrible conditions, handling toxic materials that would often result in them developing 'potter's rot', a euphemism for various forms of fatal lung disease. There was also a high level of lead used in ceramic production back then, which led to chronic poisoning that caused many miscarriages.

By the beginning of the twentieth century, women made up about half the workforce in Stoke-on-Trent's pottery factories. Conditions for all workers had improved markedly, but like all major industries, management was still dominated by men and it was near impossible for a woman to rise to a senior position. Here I'd like to talk about one notable exception: Clarice Cliff. A gifted artist, innovator and businesswoman, she was a pioneer, rising from a poor Victorian childhood to the very top of her profession, and revolutionising ceramic design along the way.

Born in 1899 in Tunstall, Stoke-on-Trent, she started work at the age of thirteen as a gilder, employed to apply thin gold lines on top of glazed ware. This requires a careful, steady hand, and young Clarice showed a real aptitude for it. As a gilder she earned a reasonable wage for a young girl, but no sooner had she mastered the technique than she left this position to join a different factory and gain experience as a free-hand painter.

This must have puzzled, and quite possibly angered, her parents, as the free-hand painting was a lower-paid job. But Clarice didn't see it that way; she simply wanted to learn the whole process of ceramic manufacturing. Instead of taking a lunch break, she would regularly explore other areas of the factory and talk to the kiln-firers, the modellers and the throwers to find out what they did and how they did it.

Aged seventeen she moved again, this time to the factory of A.J. Wilkinson in Burslem, one of Stoke-on-Trent's biggest 'potbanks' (what the locals called the pottery factories). This was seen as a very rash move, not only because it was further away from home, but because in those days, women in the pottery industry learned one task and usually remained in that position, earning the equivalent of an apprentice's wage, throughout their working life. The word 'conventional' clearly never had a place in Clarice's dictionary.

She was employed at A.J. Wilkinson as a lithographer, but during her lunch break she would go without food so she could improve her free-hand painting. One day she was spotted at this practice by a paint-shop manager, and he took her to see Colley Shorter, who ran the factory with his brother Guy. Hugely impressed by what he saw in her work, Colley immediately set Clarice to work in the design studio. This was an extraordinary promotion for any worker at that time, let alone a woman.

In 1926, when A.J. Wilkinson acquired the Newport factory next door, a tour of the new site by Clarice inadvertently led to her biggest break. She chanced upon a room filled with factory seconds that were going to be disposed of and she saw in this an opportunity to experiment and, perhaps, even save the ceramics. Because the glost ware was flawed, Clarice, with practical logic, covered the defects with a pattern of boldly coloured triangles. She undertook this project in secret over a couple of months with the help of a single paintress. What she created was truly unique, and when it was unveiled, it was given the name 'Bizarre Ware'. Not bad, eh?

Like all innovations, however, many people didn't know what to make of it. The salesman tasked with selling the new Bizarre Ware range was bewildered by it. Where to start? Colley Shorter had faith in Cliff's designs, and lent him his Rolls-Royce to transport them in. Who could resist Bizarre Ware from the boot of a Rolls? No one, it seems; the salesman's first stop was a large china retailers in Oxford, where the canny dealer bought the lot.

Clarice Cliff never looked back. In the following years, she created her celebrated Crocus Flowers pattern. All hand-painted, this vibrantly coloured range instantly attracted huge sales. She was full of ideas and always sought to push the boundaries. In 1929, she reinvented her approach to ceramic design yet again, creating geometric patterns that would later be referred to as art deco.

She was prolific, too, making around eight million pieces during her long career. Other factories paid her the ultimate compliment by producing their own version of Bizarre Ware – so many so, that she had to rebrand as 'Original Bizarre Ware'.

Her success, especially during the 1930s, was without parallel in Britain. In those days there were very few career women, and Clarice was one of a kind in her field. She ensured other talented women got opportunities working for her that they would not have got in other places: she had seventy painters, known as her Bizarre girls, and all but four were women.

Clarice Cliff, the first woman in Stoke-on-Trent to buy her own car, did not do badly for herself, or for her female colleagues.

*　　*　　*

- *I saw people who I'd worked with all them years lose their jobs and walk out the gate for the last time.*
- *It's like, did that ever happen? You know, when you see it now. Did all those people used to work here? It's like it was a dream.*
- *Whenever I walk into this factory, this is a place of wonderful memories for me, mostly happy ones and it's not memories of a general state or a place. It's individuals you remember.*

I've been visiting Stoke-on-Trent for over thirty years now. Maybe this isn't a big surprise, given its nickname is the Potteries. On every visit I would notice another factory had closed and hear people lament about how the industry there was finished. Well, it may have suffered, but it's certainly not finished, and I doubt it ever will be. Stoke is still the heart of the pottery industry in Britain, though it will never return to the 'good old days'; nothing ever does. In the nineteenth century, when more than 100,000 people from the area were employed in some element of ceramic production, factory owners must have thought the bubble would never burst.

As late as 1979, there were over 50,000 people still working in the factories that dominated the skyline of the city. But the writing was on the wall long before then. Short-sighted management and a reluctance or inability to modernise fuelled a steady decline, which globalisation then vastly accelerated, putting the final nail in the coffin of the traditional method of ceramic mass-production.

As ever, it was only ever about money; the human cost was never counted nor considered. But, you can't argue with progress. Technological advances have slowly but surely cut the work-force of every major industry over the last century. And once you're at a bare minimum, firms find an even cheaper way; they outsource production to a country where labour costs are lower, saving even more money. That's the way it goes, unfortunately.

In 1989, shortly before I left Harefield, I travelled up to Stoke with Robert and Alan. They were buying an old humidifier from a factory to take up to Scotland with them. I went along with them to help take it apart and move it. It was a huge, great old thing, about five metres by four. Or at least, I thought it was huge.

Then I was shown one of the factory's latest acquisitions in their modernisation programme, a state-of-the art tunnel kiln, over 50 metres long. It was in operation continuously, 365 days a year, day and night, I was told by the man who was in charge of it. The ware travels along a conveyor belt, gradually heating up

before being fired in the middle where the kiln is at its hottest; from there it is cooled down, reaching room temperature by the end of the cycle.

'What if something goes wrong, though?' I asked the operator, trying to find a flaw in the system.

'The computer will ring me up,' he replied.

'But what if you're not in,' I continued, still determined to find him out.

'It'll just call the next person on the list.'

I didn't push him further. It was mind-blowing, seeing how the future looked. The set-up there and the quantities produced on this endless cycle were beyond my comprehension. That was thirty years ago. Today's factories are even more sophisticated, and that is one reason there are more ceramics produced in Stoke-in-Trent today than ever before. There are merely fewer factories and fewer workers. The biggest ceramics factory in town these days is Steelite International. They produce a staggering half a million units of high-quality tableware every week for the catering and hospitality industries and sell to over 140 countries.

Back in the old days, that output would have required a workforce far bigger than the thousand or so that work there now; one that would have lived, worked and died in the neighbouring streets, themselves built by the factory owners. Now, sadly, many of those streets can be bought for the price of a family car. Workers' houses lie derelict, waiting for a developer to put them out of their misery.

Thankfully, many of Stoke's old factory buildings have been listed. Most of them will never make pottery again, but at least they will not be replaced by featureless industrial units or retail parks. But one is still making pottery, and it is less than a five-minute walk from the Steelite factory. Middleport Pottery, where we filmed *The Great Pottery Throw Down* prior to Covid-19, is still going strong over 130 years since it first opened. This is mainly down to huge support from the Prince's Regeneration Trust.

At Middleport, they still employ the old methods of decoration: hand-painting and nineteenth-century underglaze transfer printing, as pioneered at Spode all those years ago. It's a wonderful-looking complex, too: the model design for a working Victorian pottery. That was one of the main considerations when it was chosen for the *Throw Down*, I believe. It certainly looks great on camera, and I love being in the building. The atmosphere there is so full of life, industry, heritage and artistry.

I'm hopeful for the future of Stoke-on-Trent. There is too much history there for the industry simply to disappear. Potters continue to base themselves there, and there is a steady stream of new talent emerging. Over the last five or six years, I've forged a connection with Staffordshire University. Believe it or not, they even awarded me an honorary doctorate in arts, in 2019. Me: a doctor, can you imagine! Every year, they invite me to their art and design degree show, where I'm asked to judge the students' work. It's always a pleasure; the level of work I see is incredible. Not only in ceramic design, but in furniture, lighting and jewellery, too. Those students and their ideas will provide the future legacy of the city.

The Spode factory site's regeneration will take a lot of time and money, but I'm cheered by the fact that the buildings are in use and not standing empty. This also delighted the former employees who came along to the Absent Tribes exhibition in 2019. The brand lives on, too, with the Portmeirion Group continuing to produce the most popular patterns, including the Blue Italian.

Perhaps the last word should go to Alan Shenton. He started as a security guard on the site in 2002 and witnessed the final years of Spode as a working factory. He watched as his friends and colleagues, all highly skilled workers, lost their jobs in 2008. He alone remained guarding the empty shell. He was always there, bright and cheerful at the front gate, when we were putting the exhibition together.

It is his words that we used at the end of the soundscape, his voice of hope for the future of Spode and Stoke-on-Trent:

As sad as it was that the Spode site closed, it's opened a new door and people are coming back. I will happily retire when every building is occupied, you know, and I see not hundreds but thousands of visitors coming along, parking up for the day and enjoying the visit. I think that's when I'll perhaps say I can put my feet up for a bit … but not until then.

20

IT'S ALL ABOUT CONNECTION

I'm not in any way religious, but I have experienced divine intervention. Believe it or not, it was back in the summer of 1986, at a Wigs gig. We were a couple of songs into our set and a dozen or so crowd members had already cast off their shirts to slam their torsos into each other at high speed. For those of you not in the know, this meant we were going down well. Suddenly, out of the corner of my eye, I saw some bloke jump up onstage next to me and start playing the tambourine. Odd, I thought.

Turning round to check out our new member, I saw that somehow he appeared to have stepped straight out of Glastonbury Fayre circa 1971 onto our stage. His bright baggy pants were at odds with the black leather army in the audience. It unnerved me at first, but he seemed harmless – although woefully out of time.

After our set had finished, I thanked the bloke – a happy-looking soul – for accompanying us. He introduced himself as Jesus.

'What, *the* Jesus? Blimey, I thought he was dead!'

Obviously, it wasn't HIM, otherwise this would have been a very different book. But after that night, 'Jesus' would turn up regularly at our gigs and would address me by name in his mellow tones.

'Hi, Keith, good to see you.'

He was a friendly bloke, eccentric and charismatic; everyone smiled when they saw him onstage. Everyone but our drummer, that is, who always hated the fact he was out of time. Turns out 'Jesus' had been a permanent fixture on the music scene for many years. In the seventies, no festival was complete without his manic, often naked dancing. And yes, there is a famous clip of him at Glastonbury in 1971, freaking out in only a tiny green woollen tank top and nothing else. Thankfully, by the mideighties he was wearing clothes. Well, I wouldn't have wanted to see a nasty tambourine accident, or anything else.

I suppose you're wondering why, at this stage, I am bringing up this random character from my past? I will try to explain. We're getting near the end now, so bear with me one last time.

I have to admit I'd forgotten all about 'Jesus' until I was doing some research for this book early in 2021. His name cropped up when I was reliving my days in the Wigs. Curious to find out what happened to him, I typed a description of him into Google to initiate a speculative internet search. Expecting to find nothing, but hoping for some obscure article on a music website, what I turned up was a shedload of hits. The reason was immediately apparent, and not good news as I picked out several 'naked hippy dancer Jesus dead' headers. This man from my distant memory had died a few weeks before.

The *New Musical Express* had run an obituary of him, as had *The Times*, no less. Social media platforms were bursting with affectionate tributes from the countless musicians and music fans who had crossed paths with him over the years.

The articles I read were accompanied by a series of fabulous photographs of him, mostly dancing and having a high old time. Perhaps the image that best captures his essence is the most famous one. In 1999, 'Jesus' appeared on the cover of the Chemical Brothers' album *Surrender*. The artwork was based on a picture taken at the Great British Music Festival at Olympia in 1976. Virtually the whole audience is chilling out to the music, sitting cross-legged on the floor. All except one; Jesus, alone, is on his feet, leaning back, arms aloft, totally lost in the music, whatever it was.

His real name was William Jellett. He'd had a difficult early life, being taken into care aged only three and spending the rest of his childhood in a children's home. By the time he was twenty-one and living in London, he was already going to loads of gigs and telling people that he was the son of God, although he also later claimed to be the Piper at the Gates of Dawn, but that was obviously a bit too much of a mouthful. He must have mellowed somewhat as the years passed, because the 'Jesus' I knew seemed quite balanced; a bit off-the-wall, yes, but essentially someone who seemed to love life and music.

Many rumours went around about why he was called Jesus, but he performed no miracles. The handfuls of fruit and nuts he used to hand out to strangers would never multiply. He was a regular at Speakers' Corner in Hyde Park and could be seen at weekends holding his placards aloft with letters three feet high, all capitals with no punctuation. Standing on a red plastic milk crate, he would gently preach for peace and music and against meat-eating, drugs and smoking.

He danced onstage with hundreds, perhaps even thousands of bands, including some of the greats. Once during a Frank Zappa concert at Hammersmith Odeon, he'd been grooving alongside the band for so long that Frank finally said something along the lines of: 'Jesus, can you get off the stage now!' although probably not as politely. I discovered that he had a rating system for bands: if they were good he'd get his tambourine out and play along, if they were brilliant he'd reach for his maracas. Suffice to say, I never saw his maracas, but I'll still take it as a huge compliment that he thought the Wigs were worth accompanying at all.

Having thought and written about my life in some detail, I realise now that it's all about connection: with people, with places, with ideas, with the world around us. The scrawny little lad I was at St Mary's was desperately looking for something that would give his life some meaning and direction; I found that in pottery and later on with music. My original plan for this book was to deal only in those key relationships; the main events and influences in my life as I perceived them to be. I set out to write about the likes of Isaac Button and Alan and Robert, but along the way, people I hadn't considered – or had forgotten about – emerged from the shadows. Some, like Frank and Pat Radcliffe, had a direct influence on my life, while others, such as Alexandra Engelfriet, made me question and change my outlook. William

Jellett is one of those who just made me smile. Not a bad epitaph to have.

RIP, William 'Jesus' Jellett, 1948–2021.

★   ★   ★

Ironically, I don't think I've ever felt so connected as I have done during the Covid pandemic. Although my time has largely been spent with only Marj and me hunkering down at home, social media has enabled me to keep in touch with potters all across the world. Over the last year, I've been uploading video clips of me giving tips on different pottery techniques and how to avoid common mistakes. Marj filmed them as well as providing additional commentary – all off the cuff, of course – and these have become more and more popular.

With the ongoing negativity surrounding social media platforms, I'm pleased to report nothing but good, positive vibes all round. The messages and conversations the videos have prompted reflect the healthy state of pottery as a thriving craft. Figures worldwide tell us that participation has increased during the pandemic. It seems that many people, with more spare time on their hands, have developed a yearning to create things.

In fact, the current uptake in pottery and other traditional crafts owes a great deal to social media, which has helped attract a lot of younger participants. When I first went to pottery classes, I stood out as a male teenager; the rest of the class were mostly middle-aged ladies, and this is a perception pottery has found hard to shake off. Today, the younger generation is discovering that pottery is cool. They are creating their own online communities and making ceramics they can immediately post online to show off to friends and other potters. More men are taking part than ever before, which is a reflection of the positive changes that have taken place in our society, one more concerned with challenging stereotypes than bowing to macho peer pressure. It is all good.

Reflecting on this, my mind was cast back to one of the potters in the first series of *The Great Pottery Throw Down*. Nigel was a builder and I remember he was getting a hard time from his builder friends for being on the programme. Unfortunately, he was voted off in the second week, but making it onto the programme at all was a great achievement. Before he left, he gave me a beautifully delicate espresso cup and saucer that he'd made. You wouldn't have put the two together – though many have made the same observation of me over the years! It was a lovely gesture and yes, I did get emotional when he gave it to me.

Apart from sitting down at my wheel and turning out a pristine mug or plate, nothing gives me more satisfaction than being able to promote my craft and help it to reach a wider audience. The reaction to the fourth series of the *Throw Down* was particularly humbling in that respect. Once it had finished, I received so many messages from fans saying how much they had enjoyed it and that they couldn't wait for the next one.

It was screened in the middle of the third – winter – lockdown, which was by far the dreariest. To coin an even drearier phrase, lockdown meant lockdown and no one could go anywhere: not for a drink in the pub, a meal at a restaurant; some couldn't even go for a walk in the park. A British winter is long enough and dark enough as it is, but having to distance ourselves physically from friends, family and other loved ones made those months seem to drag on forever. By all accounts, we created something of a feelgood factor by bringing something positive and upbeat into people's homes among all the doom and gloom.

I think part of the appeal of the programme has been down

to the fact that although it is a competition, there has been a palpable camaraderie between the potters. They are always helping and encouraging one another. I think that was even more evident in series four, perhaps because it was filmed under lockdown conditions. In fact, with the entire cast, crew and production team isolating for the duration of the filming and having Covid tests every three days, I'd say it brought us all closer together. The ending was inspirational too, as Jodie, the overall winner, had only taken up pottery two years previously. I'm sure her success will prompt many others to give it a go. I hope so.

It seems to me that we all want to make our mark, in some way to connect with somebody or something, and to let them know we are here. The earliest civilisations left us paintings in caves, the Romans gave us underfloor heating and concrete, Prince Albert gave us the Great Exhibition and trade fairs. We've more or less covered the Earth in signs that the human race 'woz ere', so we've started to look further afield.

Ever since we've had the technology to go out into space, we've been sending stuff up there, squirrelled away in time capsules on board satellites. Partly this is because there is a hope that some aliens will find it and come down to visit, partly it's because one day the Earth will blow up and we want to leave behind evidence of our existence. Scientists believe these satellites will outlast the Earth, that they will be floating out in space when our planet is merely dust and small pieces of rock. We're talking a billion years into the future.

So, out in the cosmos, we have these space capsules and all that. And here I have an issue. I've got a bone to pick with the people in charge of choosing what goes up, whoever they are. There seems to be a gap in what they have sent up to represent our planet. I'll concede that the Golden Record, which contains images and sound recordings of life on Earth and spoken greetings in fifty-five different languages, is a joy and wholly appropriate. My favourite is in Amoy, a Chinese dialect, because it begins: 'Friends of space, how are you all? Have you eaten yet?'

No, what gets my goat is the almost total lack of pottery up there. I mean – pottery is fundamental to humanity, isn't it? From what I can gather, the only artefact currently representing my beloved craft up there is, wait for it … an Andy Warhol dick-pic drawn onto a ceramic tile. And it's the size of a postage stamp. It's on the moon, apparently. I mean, it's interesting, yes, and an Andy Warhol and all that, but … I feel what we need is some good, solid functional domestic ware up there. An intergalactic Word Range perhaps?

*   *   *

'So how's the dinner service coming on?' Marj asked me, a month or so after I started making it. Not that there was any rush; we wouldn't be entertaining at home any time soon, with lockdown restrictions forbidding it. Still, I could tell she was wondering what was holding me up. Ordinarily, I'd have been able to knock out a 32-piece dinner service in no time. But this was for us; it had to be faultless.

There was another factor that was hindering my progress: the dinner plates. In all my years of throwing, it is the plate form that I have struggled with the most. Effectively a plate, if one is making it on the wheel, is a round flat disc – the simplest of forms, but paradoxically the hardest to achieve to a satisfactory outcome, as any flaws are easily highlighted. The wide flat surface must be perfectly smooth, the rim of the plate has to be structured in such a way that the proportions are right in relation to its size, and the plate *has* to be exactly the right weight; make the base too thick and it'll be cumbersome to pick up with a plate-load of food on it. Nothing makes me more depressed than picking up a plate that is too heavy, it's unnecessary.

My main issue with plates is not so much technique, but time. In all the years I've been throwing plates to sell, it's always been up against the clock, so if I've thrown one that doesn't meet with my high standards, I have to let it go, otherwise I'd never finish the job. I'm not saying I've made terrible plates, it's that they've caused me the most anxiety when making them. I breathe a sigh of relief whenever I open a kiln full of plates to find that the rims have not slumped, the faces of the plates are flat and even, and when I pick them up, they feel just 'right'.

Making these plates for Marj, with time on my hands, I could afford to be ultra-critical and if a plate didn't pass muster, it was binned. The critical moment is after they've dried out a bit and are still leather hard. As I turn the bases of my plates, I have a good or bad feeling about them and picking them up will confirm my suspicions.

It didn't take much longer after Marj's enquiry before I had eight perfect dinner plates. Then, like small children at Christmas, we laid the whole service out on our long dining table, to see what it looked like. Marj loved it. And I was happy with my work.

One by one, I pick up the dinner plates and examine them up close, check their weight again.

They're not bad and I think to myself: You know, Jonesy, you might make a decent potter after all.

ACKNOWLEDGEMENTS

Firstly, I would like to thank my oldest and dear friend Michael James, without whose help this book would not have been so pleasurable to do, and for having the time and patience to make my ramblings into a book.

I would also like to thank Marj Hogarth, my partner, whose companionship and love certainly make this world a more fascinating and wonderful one.

Many thanks to my friend and business partner Dominic Speelman, as the journey we have both been on is in part what has brought me to this place.

Thanks also to my dear sister Sarah (aka Mrs Salideedees) and her wonderful partner Karen, for all their love and support through the good times and the not-so-good times.

I would like to thank my art teacher, Mr Mortman, for giving me my first lump of clay.

I would also like to thank my wonderfully dear friend Nia Evans for her help with the Welsh pronunciation.

Many thanks to Rupert Lancaster at Hodder & Stoughton, who is not only the publisher of this book, but was also a pottery student of mine many years ago.

… and last but by no means least many thanks to Carmen Camacho and all at Make International for their support.